P9-AOE-580

BENJAMIN

BENJAMIN

Essays in Prayer

Joseph P. Whelan, S.J.

NEWMAN PRESS
New York / Paramus / Toronto

Library of Congress
Catalog Card Number: 72-184543

Published by Newman Press
Editorial Office: 304 W. 58th St., N.Y., N.Y. 10019
Business Office: 400 Sette Drive, Paramus, N.J. 07652

Printed and bound in the
United States of America

Contents

For my Jesuit brother
and all my brother Jesuits

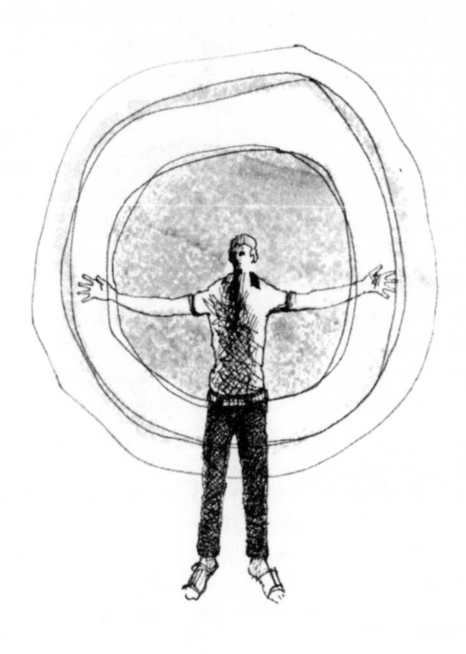

PREFACE

Benjamin is one of the great Christian names for prayer. The reader no doubt knows Benjamin's story. But I urge him to sit up close, just the same now, alert and perhaps even wide-eyed—like a child does when the story is such a good one and so well worth the re-telling that it *isn't* just an old story but is alive and new and maybe just about to happen once again—alert and ready to ask: what next? and, why? —and expecting to be surprised.

I am asking for wonder. It is a splendid gift, which is almost always being offered us—the gift of really *noticing* the massive yet detailed reality and fact of the God, and world, and men about us. But like all great gifts, especially the gift of friendship, wonder is not easy to accept and live our lives by.

The story of Benjamin is one of the earliest of the wonderful stories that lie at the beginning of God's history—that history of God, our Scripture, where our Father is story and storyteller alike.[1] God's words there, just as now, are mostly deeds—and people. Sometimes they are mighty events that work their will in an instant. Or again, and more often, they are the fragile search of a love that takes a lifetime and a world—God's lifetime in man's world—just to begin to explore itself and find a footing in the human heart.

The reader will remember. Benjamin's father was Jacob, the grandson of the promise made to Abraham that there would be a land and a people, and that God would be their—God. Man is made in God's lively and difficult, unpredictable image. Very much like God, then, and very much like all the sons of God right down to our own day, Jacob is a man of labors and of many journeys; who sojourns only fitfully, and often as a guest; and who must struggle with both God and man—struggle in the dark, beyond the evidence, and with few signals of reciprocal fidelity or life—in order just to be alive, in order just to love.

Jacob loved a girl named Rachel. He loved her well. Yet there were fourteen years—and Leah—to search and work through, and even learn to love, before Rachel came to Jacob as his own. Then a further darkness, though they are together now. It is an often difficult companionship, but Jacob and Rachel are together now to face the further darkness, before their firstborn, Joseph, comes to bless their faith. In him, in Joseph, the promise first finds flesh for *their* time and in *their* place, just as it must continue to do—find a flesh for each man and for every time that is to keep company with God and go the road with him in his journey through the world. And finally, in the shadow of Rachel's bitter death: the birth of Benjamin, who would be famous for a thousand years as symbol of man's life with God—a triumph won in Benjamin, indeed, but only through the care of Joseph and the humility of Rachel.[2]

It is not the end. For there are many further journeys still to go, deserts yet to cross, and other joys to know. Benjamin shall have to grow in wisdom, age and grace before God and toward his brothers. And so the story goes on, in the sale of Joseph into

Egypt by the sons of Leah; rises to its climax in this brother's love: Joseph's love for Benjamin; and ends with Jacob's journey into that final, adventurous peace of union with his sons—sons who shall survive him—and who shall also die—until the tale of God in the world is finally told as Christ. For *that* Word, once become flesh and world and history, shall be told, and be, forever.

I break no new ground here in seeing Benjamin as prayer, or contemplation. For the theme is a very old one. It goes back at least as far as Saint Augustine, who adumbrates the allegory of Jacob's wives, seeing Rachel as contemplation, and Leah as action.[3] The allegory gets a good deal more detailed, however, as the tradition moves along, reaching its culmination in Richard of Saint-Victor's *Benjamin Major,* but especially in the same writer's *Benjamin Minor.*[4] And the latter gets its English provenance in a racy fourteenth-century translation commonly attributed to the author of *The Cloud of Unknowing.*[5] Here, where the allegory is full blown, Jacob may be understood as God, on his journey into the human heart. Rachel, God's first love, is understood as man in his initial and preliminary spiritual dignity: his human reason. The first son born to them is Joseph (taken as discretion, or discernment), and then, and finally: Benjamin (who stands for contemplation, for that contemplative love which is wisdom). But this second birth occurs only in the course of a long journey and after much labor and fidelity. The adventure of prayer may be deeply explored here, if the story in *Genesis* is carefully attended.[6] For the deepest mysteries of Christian mysticism, as well as the relationship of mature contemplation to incarnational action, are latent in the circumstance that Rachel dies in giving birth to Benjamin, while Joseph survives and indeed plays a central role in the care and the career of Benjamin. But enough of this.[7]

I have called this book *Benjamin* for reasons that are almost wholly subjective and fond. At the same time, however, the title helps me to place the accent clearly where I want it: on contemplation. For I shall want to say that prayer simply *is* contemplation—which is what Benjamin stands for. That is, prayer is presence and companionship—however dark and troubled or however lithe and lovely this companionship may be. And this position will be a definite and, I think, easily understood rejection of the view that contemplative prayer and petitionary prayer, or mental prayer and contemplative prayer, or contemplative prayer and vocal prayer, are legitimate distinctions. Surely 'petitionary', 'mental', 'vocal', may and do speak valuably to real events that really differ. They may, therefore, be usefully distinguished among themselves. But not from contemplation. For the claim will be that specifically as prayer, they are always aspects and functions of that more fundamental drama which is the thing itself: that *companionship* and *contemplation* which all prayer essentially is.

The five chapters of this book represent, I think, rather personal and certainly only partial perspectives on the great wide world of prayer. They are in no wise systematic, therefore, nor are they especially many-sided, thorough, carefully balanced. I would hope they need not be. For however theologically reflexive, they are probably much more nearly rooted in experience and sensibility than they are in thought and research. So the reader will have his own experience to ask about and live with, as he encounters the several optics proposed for his consideration here. And in any event, this book is just one small word in a vast and often noble literature on the subject.

It is only the last three chapters that deal directly and at length with the mystery of prayer. This is deliberate. For no prayer, and certainly no Christian prayer, can be a thing apart. Prayer has—it *must* have, to be human, incarnational, Christian—a context as wide and deep as the history of man before God in the world. Of that rich and varied, constant and dynamic context, two mysteries—there are so many others—have a special prominence for me. And so I have devoted two chapters to them. The first chapter reflects upon that indwelling Spirit who prays and strives in us and whom Paul spells out as faith and hope and love. I have very much stressed that Spirit as hope. The second chapter asks about the integral paschal event itself as Cross-and-Resurrection—a process and event that is markedly history as suffering.

In concluding this preface, I would like briefly to notice that I have not apparently written about community at all—about community prayer or about the relationship of prayer to community. However, I would invite the reader to consider as we go along whether contemplation, as I shall understand it here, is not a radical condition of all community and, therefore, whether contemplative prayer is not a radical condition of all Christian community. I intend nothing very complex by this statement. For by community I mean simply a *congregati in unum,* that is, a number of persons significantly gathered together in terms of an ideal, a project, a commitment—or God. But the 'unum', whatever it is, cannot simply be *known,* I would think, by the several persons involved, as a piece of information they might share, or as a fact they might agree on. Nor can it just be responded to casually, speculatively, theoretically. No, community takes passion and commitment. The 'unum' in question must be continually, emotionally interiorized, actualized, existentialized, experienced and *lived*. It must happen. That is to say, it must be contemplated. Otherwise, you will have at most a group. It may be a pleasant group, or maybe it will bicker, or be vague, fragmented, ineffective. But it will not be a community unless there is this contemplation, this *human* appropriation into one's flesh and blood of the 'unum' in terms of which the members gather—in terms of which the members are gathered. All community, if this is the case, whether it be political, marital, or whatever, demands such contemplation. And since God, God in Christ, is the 'unum' in terms of which all *Christian* persons gather and love and work, then Christian community will demand that *kind* of contemplation which is prayer. It is just this contemplative prayer, and explicitly seen as radical condition of community, which occupies me in this book.

I want to thank my editor, Mr. Richard J. Payne, for his suggestions about the format of this book. And I want to thank too Mr. John T. Polk, S.J., for the great assistance he has given me in reading and preparing the manuscript and proofs.

Joseph P. Whelan, S.J.
6 August, 1971
Feast of the Transfiguration

I
INTRODUCTORY TO PRAYER

1.
Faith and Hope and Love

The chosen focus of this essay—as just one possible prolegomenon to prayer—is hope. But the more precise subject of our concern here is

hope in its relation to faith and love,
hope as an inner moment of one dense experience.

There are wholly adequate reasons
for the distinction of faith and hope and love.
But the risk is run that we shall separate
what we mean only to distinguish.
Things may sometimes be separated into their parts
with good results.

But faith-hope-love is not a thing.
It is a life. It is Christian life.
And while life, as dynamic and historical,
has aspects, moments and movement,
it does not have parts. It is not a thing.
To separate life from itself is to kill it.

Further, faith-hope-love is not a problem,
which may also have parts
whose proper arrangements can lead us to answers.
Rather,

faith-hope-love is a mystery,

to be penetrated and experienced.
It is alive, a summons to awe and to action
—to let it be, let it be so, to let it happen.
The task is response, to be sure,
but the called-for response
is not so much answer as *affirmation*
of what God has said and done,

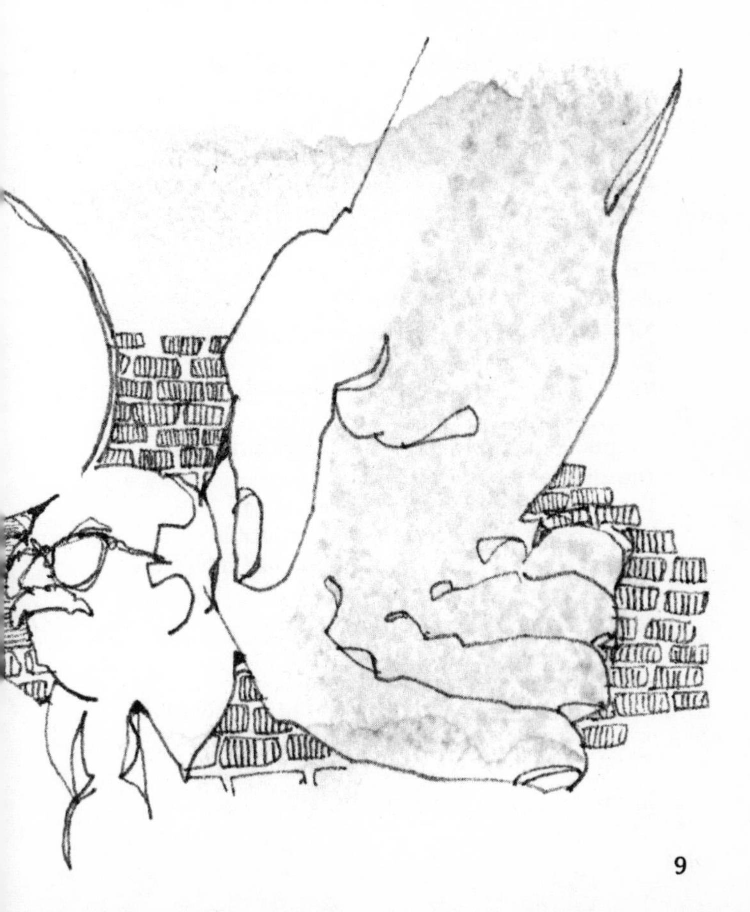

of what he is doing,
and the appropriation of his deed as my own.

Ultimately, ideally, at the end,
I am what he is doing.
I am God's deed done in Christ whom I become,
through their Spirit,
in the Church.
To separate mystery from itself,
to attempt its parts, is not to solve mystery
but to impoverish and perhaps to destroy it.

So we treat faith and hope and love,
together and in their distinction,
as the one deed of God: the Christian life,
which is the mystery of Christ.
And not just any Christ.
But the one who is alive.

in the growing body of his resurrection.

Faith and hope and love
as a formula for the Christian style of life
is a characteristically pauline expression.
It names the three great charismata
which constitute the people of God
and which also mark each man
as numbered among that people.
Paul is well aware that the body of Christ
has many parts, a plurality of members,
and the hands are not the feet,
nor are the eyes the ears.
But the body is one and exists
from a single principle of life, the Holy Spirit.

So too among just fellow men and Christians.
The differences are real.
The gifts are as wide and as various
as the needs and tasks, and as irreducible
as the breadth and reach of the human adventure
under victorious grace.
Yet the adventure is seen finally to occur
under *one* grace, one Holy Spirit
who is the bridal gift of the risen Lord
to a Church become the beloved of his own flesh
through the gift bestowed.

So the many gifts are one gift.

And the one gift is faith and hope and love.
And finally, just the greatest of these,
which is love.[1]

Paul can say this last because,
both on the part of the initiating God
and of responding man,
love is the total fundamental act
which integrates everything else.
Yet as Rahner notices,
this love must declare itself in history
in a multiplicity of actions
distinct though not separate from each other
and from love.

Faith and hope give love a concrete presence
in the world. They test love
and are both source and fruit of its growth
and strength. And so Paul urges his readers
to 'put on the breastplate of faith and love,
and for a helmet the hope of salvation'.
He prays for his readers and gives thanks,
'remembering before our God and Father
your work of faith and labor of love
and steadfastness of hope in our Lord Jesus Christ'.[2]

'In our Lord Jesus Christ'.

This brings us to the central statement we shall have to make in this essay.

Faith-hope-love is a person, Jesus Christ.
These three are not just *about* Christ
as their source, their motive and their goal
—though they are most surely and importantly
this too.
But prior and more fundamentally,
faith and hope and love are the primary grace itself
—incarnational, incarnated grace:

> God our Father's victorious and absolute gift
> of himself
> through Christ in the Holy Spirit to men.

Faith, hope and love are what God is and does.
And they are what *we* are, when we become Christ,
sons in the Son.
And they are what we do, when we do

what Christ does: cry Abba! Father, in the Spirit.
And they are (but carefully here,
for how can man *have* God?) what we have,
when we have the mind and heart of Christ,
the Spirit himself.[3]

The mystery deepens when we stress this theme
of person,
and it reminds us that a life, the life of God,
is what Paul haltingly attempts to verbalize
when he speaks of faith and hope and love.
The words bristle with tension,

for they speak properly of at least three inner moments of God the Father's encounter with man through Christ in the Spirit. And each of these moments or levels of the mystery reveals in turn the rich overlapping and unity of faith and hope and love.

In the first place, God is not man.
Here, God as my faith, my hope and my love
is precisely what I am not.
Distance is experienced, and it is real.
This God is not given, but proposed.
And the self-disclosure says fidelity to a promise
of agapeistic love which shall have to re-create
my sinful self, my not-self,
to new lovableness, new being, in Christ.

Here, I am invited, summoned.
But I am free.
Not free to believe and hope and love.
That must be given me. That must be done in me,
for me, by this Lover
who must create my availability and my response.
My freedom just here is negative.
I may not say yes, but I may say no.

I am invited to believe and trust
that the Father's powerful love
as displayed and offered in the weakness of Christ
has utterly altered my hope.
Distance is shattered, on God's side,
and it is revealed that

there is a future for me and my world,
which I may risk.

For Christ's resurrection in flesh
is the declaration of human eternity.

Belief in Christ's resurrection creates the hope
that I and the world I build
may be loved forever.
And, in Christ,
be worth the love.

The distance has been real here
and speaks of a journey.
But God in Christ
present and offered to man in the Church
is a journey already taken,
and a distance overcome.

The second inner moment of faith and hope and love
finds this God who is not man
as the God who is in man,
the God who is in the world.
We may call this grace, but we ought to mean
something wonderfully forceful by it, if we do.

For we have to mean nothing less
than the Spirit of the Son, ardently trusting
the Father's old promises massively kept
in Christ's resurrection,
which now grounds anew this same Spirit's
invincible hope that all Christ's brothers
and the world Christ loves
shall see in their own risen bodies
what they may know now in faith
and may run toward with certain hope:
their adoption in love.

Here once again,
faith and hope and love are not what man is,
nor are they what man does. Here as before,
it is God who is faith and hope and love.
Paul is absolutely clear on this.
It is the Spirit who groans and prays.[4]
We are saved by his hope, by his faith and love.

Yet something new and marvelous, all the same,
is afoot. For what was just call

and summons and demanding disclosure
is now also response.
And while the response of faith and hope and love
remains of God and by God,
it has become nonetheless a human
and worldly reply.
For at least as regards our universe,

> the Spirit, who is love,
> shall always be a *man's* love
> when the never-to-be-discarnate Son
> tells his Father:
>
> I love you.

And the Spirit abroad in the world
through the Church
is a brother's gift to his brothers,
a gift won by an almost scandalously human hope.
For it was beyond all evidence
that Jesus trusted his Father to love him
faithfully.

In both Jesus and his brothers, then,
the summons and self-disclosure of God
as faith and hope and love has a reply.
And while it is God himself, the Holy Spirit,
and not man, who makes, who is that reply,
yet the Spirit's yes to the Father through Christ
—at this second level of the mystery we are treating—

> is made in man and for man,
> and if not by him,
> yet not without him.
>
> For here, God has been given to God
> in history, which makes it a human event.

And man's freedom grows.
Where before man could only refuse to say no,
now a fundamental affirmation occurs.
Man does not yet say yes in himself,
but the way and the means to that moment are here
in the believing and loving,
in the ardently hoping Spirit within him.

Here God *is* given, and *because* he is received.
The Spirit in man has made men Christ-ian,
for the Spirit is the Father's gift of himself,

which is Christ.
And the Spirit in man has made men sons,
for he is in man

as Christ's improvident trust and certain hope
across death itself of requited love:
Abba! Father.

If a journey remains to be made,
yet the mystery presses to paradox.
For this journey is seen now
to be a march into the here,
with eyes on a future that has come.

We move toward death as risen men,
in the resurrection of Christ.

Hope tumbles over faith now and somersaults
before love.
For hope is at once source and fruit of trust,
and it gives the sharp edge to that love
which is desire leading to act.
Its certainty produces a patience
with respect to him who has not yet come,
and at its finest,
hope dissolves into the silence of a restless joy,

because he who is coming is here.

The third inner moment or level of the mystery
of faith and hope and love
as the personal encounter of God and man
concerns what man is, who he becomes,
what he may do,
given God's word of disclosure (the first inner
moment),
and the gift of God himself through Christ
in the Spirit (the second).

This God who is not man,
yet who in Christ has become man,
and who by his Spirit indwells men,

lets this love affair get out of hand.

Out of his hands, and into ours.
And we become him, and do what he does.
For the humanity of God I share

is not just something I have, however gratefully.
The humanity of Christ is what I am,
it is what I do.
And the world with which he is eternally involved
and part of whose matter is forever his flesh,
is my world. And my work affects it.

To go further and farther.
Love is creative of itself in another,
for love is a gift of being and being of act.
And so the Spirit of Christ
abroad in the flesh of the brothers of Christ
creates an aftermath and a future

which is me
and what I may thus hope to become.

The Spirit is *memory* of promises made,
believed on, and kept.

And he is the *future,*
my hidden Lord hoped on and well on the way.

And the Spirit is also that joy,
or often fierce peace, that grapples these two
in the *present* possession of love.

And these three are mine, are who I am, what I do.
It is I who believe and hope and love.

The Spirit has come (the second inner moment
of the mystery), and has made all things new.
And this last is the third inner moment,
the new creation, which I am, which I do.
For if, with Paul, it is not I but Christ who lives
and acts in me,
so too again with Paul, it is I who live
and act in him,
uttering through him in the Spirit
the great Amen of my faith and hope and love.[5]

God divinizes me in Christ,
God's word is deed of me in Christ.

For it is not so much that God gives himself
to me in Christ,

as that he gives me to himself in Christ.

With all the richness of its ambiguity,
man is a gift of God.

Mary of Nazareth found words for the deed of God
which was, in direct proportion to its being God's,
her own.
Her history gives flesh
to the three inner moments of faith and hope
and love,
where grace and human freedom rise and fall together.
And the movement issues
in the pride of a superb, legitimate
and fully human exaltation, whose roots
are the most awesome creaturely humility.

Her sinlessness and virginity are God's own work:
an availability—which she does not refuse—
for a possible encounter
which is entirely up to him:

'Let it happen to me'.

And so the Spirit is within her,
giving that reply to the Father which is Christ.
And then it is
that the gift of God which is yet a human,
worldly accomplishment, occurs.

> *Because* God has done mighty things in her,
> *she* shall do a deed the generations will
> remember:
>
> a woman, and not God, is the mother of God.

Christ here is a worldly achievement
and the foundation of Christian secularity.

Faith, hope and love coalesce to the stillpoint
of a passivity that is wholly in action:
God, given by God to man, in Mary's virginity,
becomes the God-man given by man to God and men,
through her motherhood.[6]

We have here also the image of the Church
as bride, as body and as mother.

Because the Church has *received* Christ,
she may *become* him and *give* him to men
—and to God.
The Church too is faith and hope and love
on the three levels we have been treating:

God as summons and demanding self-disclosure:
the Lord of the Church;

the Spirit constitutive of her unfailingly
holy response: the Lord within the Church;

and the fruits of the Spirit,
which, even as they measure the scandal
of her sinfulness, also become the flesh
of her mission to the world
and her human achievement in building
the larger body of Christ's resurrection
against the Day of his Father.[7]

What does this Church, what does Christian man
hope for?
He hopes for faith, which of course he already has
if his hope is Christian at all,
but yet which though given remains gift on the way,
an object of hope, something and someone
approaching,
or, better, moving forward ahead of man,
beckoning him on into a world of movement
and growth.

Man hopes to believe what the future will show
Christ to be.
He hopes to trust this Other
who enters his present to lead him beyond it.
And he hopes to greet this encounter with love.

Rahner suggests that New Testament hope is ultimately
the intersection, on the one hand, of God's love
become human history in Christ and, on the other,
the confident response of man who awaits, with the
certainty of faith, the final consummation of that
love, which is the coming of Christ.

Man hopes then in God, in love,
and in nothing else.

But he hopes in God's love
as revealed in God become history, Christ,
and as revealed in the total, the corporate Christ,
where resurrection is for the moment
mediated in passion,
and life is the meaning of death.

So man hopes in the world and in his brothers
and in the promise to be kept
that is himself.

Hope here is the product of a faith
that his corporate history,
which is still man's becoming,

already exists in Christ.

And hope here is the edge on man's love,
impelling him to make Christ's history his own.
Father William Lynch wisely warns against
the disastrous and unchristian consequence
of hoping for the impossible.
It is to skirt the definite, and to fly the real.
It is gnostic, and it invites despair.

God given to God by man.
Absurd? Impossible? Pelagian?
That depends on just how far
man's Lover wants to go and to what prodigal
extent his love has willfully got out of hand.

God's love, God's love for man in Christ
must be the Christian measure of the possible.

Here once again, *faith*
gives the dimensions of realistic hope,
of what man may hope to love.
The love of God revealed to faith
in the Father's entire gift of himself in Christ
suggests the size of the reply
that man and his world may hope to make
to the Father through Christ in the Spirit.

There is a dialectic and tension throughout.
Christ has died once and for all,
putting sin to death. And his resurrection
is communicated in the human history
which is his Spirit abroad in the Church

and in the world of men through baptism.
And yet man sins.
And if Christ's death was not for a while
to be the end of death, but the creation
of the possibility of *Christian* death,
yet man does die.
He hopes to be with God in a risen life
he does not yet have.
Man hopes for what he does not wholly have.
The last times are here, and are yet to come.[8]
Where then is the center and the focus
of the hope man ought to have this day?

Hope has a memory and a dream.
It lives from the past and draws on the future
for a present task and a work at hand: love.
Hope remembers, and this is its faith:

the eternity of God and the resurrection of Christ.

As simple as that.
But as Father David Stanley notices,
New Testament memory is never nostalgic,
never harking back to the good old days.
The Church's hope is the risen Lord,
present even as he strides ahead of us,
and yet who is coming soon:
maranatha![9]
And this last is the dream of hope, its future:

the Lord who is coming very soon.

And this dream is as idealistic as the love
of all the lovers who ever hoped to be one forever.
But the dream of Christian hope is not sentimental.
Rather it is brutally realistic,
creating the future out of the past facts
of a very certain faith.
Christian hope is a phoenix born of a bloody death
and an empty tomb eleven apostles died for.
And yet they did not die for a death
and an empty grave,

but for a resurrected Christ.

And this leads on to love,
love which is always of the present,
engaged with the One who is, and who is here.

Out of the memory and the dream which is its faith,
hope structures the content
and forges the *élan* of present love.
Hope gives love brilliance, and patience,
and the heart for suffering.

It gives to love love's other name:

> joy,
> the possession of hope's
> own expectations.
> Hope gives love the truth
> to be loved in faith.

Man ultimately wants, he is ultimately made for,
nothing but love:

> to love and to be loved, worthily, with fidelity,
> and forever.

This is Christian man's hope,
for which he can give good account.[10]
His hope is an anchor[11] sunk deep in the ground
of Christ's resurrection,
and it is also flung into the future
of his own resurrection and life
that is already present
in the Lord who is coming soon,
man's own resurrection and life which,
in the Spirit, is emphatically here,
made present and real in faith. Eternal life
is in history. Man's salvation by faith
is made present in hope.

And man loves accordingly, *now*.
Hope is to act in love *now*
according to the full dimensions of easter faith.
It is to love my brothers now,
to love this world now, and to be loved, now,
as they and I shall be, because in faith I know
we now are, already risen in Christ, truly lovable
and loved,
already hidden with Christ in God.[12]

> It is only the glory that has yet to be revealed.

Hope is to treat my brother,
as he appears now,
according to what my faith
says he shall one day be
and, in Christ,
already is.

And all this is the eucharist,
born of a past made present in faith,
pledge of a future hope
that is already here as suffering and celebration
in the deeds of men who love.

We had sung to us, some time ago,
a song of *Yesterday,*
when 'love was such an easy game to play.
All my troubles seemed so far away.
Now I need a place to hide away.
Oh I believe in yesterday'.
Here, man believes only the evidence,
which is to have no faith at all
and no foundation for risk.
And the evidence is death,
which is the end of hope.
For love has died. And the memory of love
is memorial only, a locket for our loss.
Memory here is not a sacrament,
and so there is no eucharist.
It is a wise song, and realistic,
whose hope is at one with its faith.
It is the *sperabamus,* the 'we were hoping'
of the two disciples whose footsteps
are dogged toward Emmaus.[13]
Man here is being toward death.
Love is phosphorescence and hope has no dreams,
but only a memory of life, and the evidence
of death.
It is nostalgia, which in its pure state,
however languidly and sentimentally devised,
is the inverse of hope,
having the structure of despair.

Yesterday.
If Christ is not risen, then he is only yesterday.
He is not today and forever,

and we are still in our sins.[14]
We are men without hope
who have no God in the world.[15]
And ultimately, there will be no one to love.

But if I believe in Christ's resurrection
from the dead,
then he is alive today and forever for me,
not just as value or milieu, but as Person.
And my hope may summon out of the future
which already is in him,
the *entire* mystery of Christ.
I move toward my own death and my own risen life,
and that of my brothers, and of the world too,
as coming and as present in him.
My hope has seized upon the entire expanse
of what faith says history is and shall be

—I take the risk
of what this history shall turn out to be,

in faith that it has occurred in him,
and so is available *now* for my response.

And so I may love now,
even as I serve their weakness,
my already risen brothers;

I may love now,
even as I strenuously build,
our already re-created world
—risen and re-created now, if hiddenly,

in the present, if hidden Lord of glory.

Hope makes present
the whole Christ whom faith makes real,
and offers his final beauty
to the present service of man's love.

2.
Salvation through Suffering

The primary and the finally important things that ought to be said about man, and about each one of us, are not problems. What man fundamentally is, what he does, what happens to him—these are not problems. For they are not available to man for adequate analysis or definitive solution. They lie too deep for that.

Man, at the roots of his being and his action,
where he stands partner to his world,
his fellows and his God,
is a mystery.
And while we do, or may hope to one day, solve
all our problems, we do not
—whatever the jacket of the bestseller
'whodunnit' may say—solve mysteries.

We ponder mystery, we entertain it,
we try to formulate and structure it ever and anew.
We criticize our past attempts to do so,
and begin again, or further build
on what seems adequate.
But the aim is not solution.
The aim and the task

is to keep the mystery integral and immediate,

so that the mind may recognize and be seized
with its importance,
that the heart may become involved in its beauty,
to the end that man,
in his social entirety as person in the world,
may *experience the reality*
of which the mystery speaks
—and respond.
Respond to the mystery of himself, his world,
and his God.

No mystery tackles the heart of man so frontally,
or tempts so much his faith to scandal
—his faith in himself and in his God;

and no mystery rages in his prayer so greatly,
or so greatly threatens whether there *can,* or *need,*
or *shall* be such a thing as prayer

—as does the mystery of suffering.

And none has cast more doubt upon the nature
of salvation or the value of this world.

We may deliberate a moment, then,
on these two aspects of one mystery.
But we deliberate a *mystery.*
We seek to clarify, and not to solve,
the salvific suffering of man.

Every man receives the mystery of suffering once.
The Christian does so twice, at least theoretically.
All will depend on whether the second encounter
remains an idea only, or becomes *experienced,*
as the first must be.

For every man finds the mystery of suffering
thrust upon him,
carved into the marrow of his own bone and spirit.
And if he is a great lover,
he will confront it even more fearfully
in the tears of others. Man may not opt
for or against suffering. It is there,
and is no abstraction, but a battering experience
whose history man fears
and whose future he can count on.

This does not prevent, however,
there being several ways of taking thought or act
against the mystery of pain.

It can be denied that suffering is mysterious at all. And this in two ways. Suffering can be reduced to a problematic—an *unsolved* problem, to be sure. An unbelievably formidable problem, perhaps, maybe never to be completely answered or controlled. But the quotients are at least theoretically within man's reach, eventually, if he will persevere. Such a view is probably not common,

take us man for man.
The farther reaches of the heart

give the lie to such a hope.
Our public philosophies, of course,
are quite another thing.
And there we see only apparently strange bedfellows,
from Rousseau, through Marx and Nietzsche,
until now.
And on this far more superficial level,
we most of us pitch in,
and lead our slight, disintegrated lives.

There is another view of suffering that also denies to it the quality of mystery. But here, suffering is not a problem either. It does not become a question

which goes as yet unanswered,
but which may be progressively explored.
Rather it is seen as a question
to which there *is* no answer, anywhere.
And that is contradiction.
Suffering is experienced, then,
neither as mysterious nor problematic,
but as absurd.

And man and world,
through whom pain makes its mute and grinning way,
are nonsense too. Tragic nonsense.
The appropriate response to such a chaos
will be endurance, or despair.
And one may argue about which is apposite,
and about nothing else.
There need be nothing superficial in this view.
And the courage of its unbelief,
the integrity with which it often lives
with its conclusions—where not some aesthetic
stance of fashion—
should give a Christian pause.

A final view of suffering apart from Christ—and possible, it would seem, only to some degree of faith, however primitive—fully affirms the mystery. Here too there are no answers (and Christianity will show small difference at this point). But there is little insight either

into the relationship of suffering and love.
(And it is just here
that Christianity will explode within the spirit
of the man of faith,

if anything *even further darkening* his *mind*
to the mystery
by the very *light* and fullness of its revelation,
even as it enlivens his heart
by the beauty of its promise.)

What *is* affirmed in this inchoate revelation,
whether 'natural' or historical, and what is
bravely fought for, is the conviction
that the answer to the mystery of suffering
does exist,
that it is compassed within the integrity
and wisdom of Another,
and that this Other can be trusted.

The splendid effort of the heart
involved upon this trust
is classically displayed in that most impatient
of the scriptures, the Book of Job.
Man fairly shouts there for a further revelation,
for a *larger* mystery,
that will deepen even as it clarifies
a larger wager yet.
Man asks for justice in the Book of Job
as he seeks escape from pain.
But it will be his blessed fortune
the request is swept aside, for that way
lies only death. The Lord of life,
in his own good time, will reply instead with love,

> with gracious favor that is purely gift.
> He will respond with self-donation,
> which is the deepest etymology of love.

And this will mark a second,
quite notably Christian, stance
before the mystery of suffering: [1]

> Life that dies in agony,
> that we may die no more;
>
> Joy that grieves unbearably,
> for the building of our peace.

Sin, the sin of the world, the sins of each man and his responsibility for them, the idea of sin and its historicity, man's experience of sin and his belief in it:

all this is not our topic here. We simply accept it as a fact.

Sin, especially for Saint John, is hate.
It is disunity, rupture, it is to be at odds,
apart from, to walk another way.
It is the distance and estrangement Adam knew
at once and to his shame before God
and toward his wife.
Alienation is not just the effect of sin.
It is the thing itself as well.

It is the decision of Cain to walk apart from Abel.

And man's instinct ever since
has been to classify his world, in order
to divide and separate, whether by color, creed,
or economics.

Sin is also the separation, the rupture,
within the man himself

> —the lie the mind tells to the heart,
> the betrayal of the spirit by the flesh
> or, conversely,
> the denial of affectivity and flesh
> by an arrogance of spirit.

Even in the beauty of our human loves,
we catch the rhythm and the footfall
of our sickness unto death.
The very goodness of our lives
is shadowed by the curse that we have dealt us.
What greater grief than 'goodbye'
to those we truly love.
It is our sin, that even stalks our innocence,
taxing it with suffering, with loneliness,
and death.

In Jesus Christ the Godhead enters history.
Not in effective power merely, like the first time.
But in Person.
The Godhead takes upon itself a history
and a world.
God does not destroy that history or that world.
But he confronts it with himself, for what he is.
And God is love.

God is that situation, that condition of Persons
who are completely at one, who are perfectly
and endlessly together, present to one another
in mutual self-surrender.
For the revelation of Christ's divinity
is specified.
He is not thrust into our history as our God merely.
He is revealed to us and *for* us
as our God the Son, the Son of a most loving
Father.
And the love, the self-donation, that is given
and received between them
is a Gift so joyous and complete
that it is a Person like and equal to themselves:
the Holy Spirit of Father and of Son.
The trinitarian Godhead is an unending adventure
of delight, the eternal presence to each other
of Lover and Beloved, in and through their community
of Love.

As such, this love affair breaks in
upon our history, our history of sin,
as we have so briefly told it,
our world of shattered loyalties
and distant looks,

our land of Cain that lies far east of Eden.

Our world, in a word, of hate.

We would expect the confrontation
of these milieux of hate and unconditioned love
to be drastic and explosive. And it is.
In one man, one of our own, Jesus Christ,
this love affair takes on our world of hate,
not to contract its guilt, but to forgive it,
and to assume its grievous aftermath of suffering,
of loneliness, and death.
God did not remain overagainst man in a posture
of condescending mercy.
He became man. He took on the flesh of sin.
He became it,

and then forgave it in himself,
Jesus Christ.

And since Christ's flesh was ours,
God forgave us in and through his Christ,

that we might then forgive ourselves, bless
one another, and our world.
Forgiveness is but this: to reconcile, to reunite.

The Incarnation is a friendship,
nothing else, and that's salvation.

It is atonement too, the walking together,
the being-at-one, of God and man,
of man and man, the flesh and blood now,
the brothers of Christ.
And finally, as man had given Christ his flesh,
so Christ gives man his Spirit. Brothers
become sons, who may say: Abba! Father.

This is salvation. It is a fact for one man, Jesus Christ. For the rest it is a possibility. The salvation of Jesus Christ reaches its victorious and brave conclusion in the very enactment of his passage to the Father.

But it was a road to go, a passage to be made.

The johannine theology of the crucifixion is marvelously precise. The salvation of the Son of God who is now also Son of Man, the coming together of Lover and Beloved—the end of loneliness and hate—all this occurs at the very moment of dereliction and of death. Saint Mark's Christ cries out the most unbearable words a man has ever said:

'why have you forsaken me'.

He was alone—which turned out to be union.
And then he died—which turned out to be life,
and perfect love.

'He handed over his spirit.' Which may mean: he died; and also: he gave his Father all the love he had: the Holy Spirit; and then again: *with* his Father, he poured out that Spirit upon all men, bringing to birth his bride the Church in a community of love with himself and of all men with each other.

This happened to the Man. He suffered,
and was saved. It is available to men,
a *possibility*. For love is a freedom, a gift,
and a wager too.

There is a road to go, a passage to be made.

It is the very structure of the lukan gospel.
There is a journey to be made—a suffering—
and by and through it lies the entrance
into glory.
Salvation is an exodus, a trek from introversion
into communal existence.
And there are no options here.
There is just his way to walk, his truth to trust,
and just his life to live. Yes, or no.
The Father has only one Word to say,
one Deed to do: Jesus Christ.
There is just one altar, one victim, one priest.
Christ's work is done, is being done,
and its effect remains: it is salvation
wrought by pain.
And we are bid, in both liturgy and life,
to follow and repeat, in effective commemoration.
Yes, or no.

And here we face our fact.
The salvation of the world by Christ is had
through suffering, loneliness and death
—and resurrection.
This alone is what saves us.
Not life alone, nor death alone either.
But pain and death for the sake of life.
We are taught here with a not-to-be-evaded clarity,
but with no questions asked or answered,

> what is and shall be the meaning of love,
> and what the cost of hate:
>
> it is a *pierced* and gloriously risen Christ
> who is and shall remain forever
> the apple of his Father's eye.

Suffering, loneliness, death, and resurrection.
It is an impenetrable mystery.
But it is the rhythm of the human heart
forever now, and no man may skip a beat.
Why? why? Why could not Love forgive,
and then let be? Why could not Love
astonish and defeat our petty hate,
except by suffering and loneliness and tears,
by most awful sorrow unto death?
Why could Life not conquer death except by dying?

Why could it not? Perhaps it could.
Why did it not? Oh there are human reasons,
and some fair ones, why love chose to go so far.
The Old Testament is crowded with shadows
of what Christ will do, with Isaac,
and the covenant that Yahweh struck with Israel
by having Moses sprinkle spilt blood on the altar
and the people,
to signify the union and new friendship
of the living God and man. And Paul
picks up the theme. It tells what Christ will do,
and what his deed effects.
But it does not finally tell us why, why Christ
had to suffer,

why love went that far.

It is a mystery, the most appalling
and most beautiful of our race:
a divine and suffering messiah, who died for love.
I do not *understand* this love,
or why he had to die. But I *know* it,
I *experience* its dark and necessary beauty.
And I am asked to follow. 'Master, where
do you live?'

'Come and see.'

He died for our sins, and rose for our justification. And Paul goes on. We are baptized into his death, buried with him by baptism into death, and by his resurrection, we walk in newness of life.

We are baptized into the death and resurrection
of Christ: salvation through suffering.
The deed of God in Christ,
and our baptism into it,
transforms the world, the world of men and trees,
the city and the tomb. It is a new creation,
alive to God, become one in the human flesh
of Christ.

The deed of God in Christ
is a revolution in the universe,

an end and a wholly new beginning.
It is a victory that destroys defeat itself.
And the baptismal waters of death and life

build us into that victory of Christ,
and through him, into one another.
In him we all, together,
make our passage to the Father,
where friendship is, salvation.

But baptism is not a magic moment
that destroys our history and time,
nor does it shatter our psychology.
The Son of Man regards our time and place
most seriously.
And it is a history of sin as well as love,
a fugue of hate, with all the suffering consequence
that jostles us each day.
Salvation kills our sin, our hate,
but not its consequence: salvation
is no twinkling of an eye.
Our sin and hate took time. They have a history
and a structure in our flesh and our psychology,
and in the world about us.
Our *love* must have a history too.
Christ's love did:

> there was a road to go, a passage to be made.
> No twinkling of an eye.

The victory of Christ will never be gainsaid.
But it will have a history.
Our evil shall be allowed to test it,
and our suffering augment it, as Paul says,
in his magnificent and startling boast
to the Colossians.

> And the Lord within the Church, the Holy Spirit,
> will groan and grieve,
> and know but little ease.

Salvation is Christ's love for us,
it is his Holy Spirit offered to our freedom.
In us, in each one of us,
Christ makes his passage once again,
a million billion times, as many times
as there are men to make it,
if we will have it so.
Through suffering and loneliness, to death
and resurrection.
And we are one Christ now, all of us,

built into the body of his death and life,
one fellowship of friends.

And so we go the road together.

Yet we are one man too, each one of us,
with a burden and a promise of our own.
And the passage will be definite,
with details of horror and of beauty

that will face the Christ in each of us alone.

Suffering, then, is ingredient to the mystery
of Christ.
Yet we must not sentimentalize it.
It is a thing to fear and dread.
Christ was a teacher in Israel with powerful gifts
of mind and heart and personality,
who desperately wanted to succeed and to be happy.
We mock the *man* if we say less than that.
And suffering sent him grovelling to the earth
in sweating panic
in the very hour of his glory.
Suffering is an evil, and the aftermath of hate.

Yet the superb intelligence of God in Christ
found its irrational terrors
a fruitful passage back to his own love.

We raise our fist at it,
which is a human thing to do.
The Lord was moved once to knock the chalice
from his Father's hands.
But we must not curse it. Suffering lies deep
in the ground of our Christian hope,

like grain in April.

It is a mystery of God.

Our talking of salvation needs precision, for there is a difficulty and a danger in our metaphor of 'passage'. The resurrection of Jesus Christ, his coming to life again in the friendship of his Father's love, is our salvation. It is the term of a passage that we have briefly sketched: suffering, loneliness, death—and resurrection. And we follow Christ in this.

But what of *time* for Christ?
What of his history as a man who loved and ate
and slept, who grieved for Lazarus?
What of the laughter and the work of this carpenter
who lent his hands and strength,
as men are called to do,
to the building of man's city here on earth?
Was this salvific for himself, for us?

The question is not: did his life contribute to the salvation that was perfectly wrought in his death and resurrection? We know it did. The question rather is:

was work well done worth doing for itself,
was his grief and laughter
part of the Kingdom of God, or only
a preparation for it?
Did the last times in any sense enter history
with him? Did he share as man, even *then,*
at least at times, his Father's love and joy?
Or did salvation consist wholly
in his final resurrection?

If so, then the passage itself,
the suffering and loneliness and death,
is *only* a means and not a part of love
which is salvation.

It is a way to love, but is not love.
This earth is a way, and not a place.

Or is the *whole* of Christ's life
fraught with the energy and integrity
of his final triumph,
so that it seeds with eternity all he is and does,
his tears and his most glancing smile,
his casual dislikes and his 'worldly' loves?
And not in theory only,
or in a truth known only to dark faith.

Did he *experience* salvation
while he was still among us,
at least from time to time? Did it happen to him
then, or was time just for pain and waiting?
Was there love,
were there friends and fellowship,
stumbling certainly, but often splendid,

and did he leap for the joy of it,
even then?

And what of us,
who live in the gift-time of the resurrection,
the *kairos* of the Spirit?
What of our world, our material world,
a part of which is forever the risen flesh
of the only Son of God?
Is life only a time of waiting and of suffering

—a waiting strengthened by the Spirit—
with love and unity, salvation, appended
as a hope? Is the world till now
still just a place of beauty and deceit,
to test and baffle us, the battleground
of a victory that lies completely beyond history?
What is salvation? When?

There are three large possibilities. Let us draw their broadest simplest lines, as we conclude. We may even caricature a bit, to make the options clear. The differences rarely will be dogmatic ones. They will occur more generally in the emphases and structures given to that dogma as it gets articulated and applied in both theology and life. The effects are especially apparent on the emotional level, where they should be, on the level of *action* and *piety*—which makes them of great importance.

A view of over-riding influence in our history sees salvation as substantially

a reality of the future life alone.
Baptism here is the forgiveness of sin,
which is a negative truth, and a great one.
Baptism is not *experienced,* however, as salvation,
but more as a pledge of it and a promise
of the means to acquire it.
Salvation is a standard to be attained,
not a presently available situation
to be entered into (a very ascetical, thoroughly
non-mystical view of man in the world before God).
This world and all our human loves are good,
but thoroughly dangerous. Experience
will largely show them to be ashes in the mouth.
The eternal God of the vision of the blessed
is man's one true desire. He is salvation,
or rather, will be—*then,*
awaiting us at death with his reward.
The world and all our human powers—notably
our bodies—are opportunities and temptations.
They are effectively *means,* occasions
for penitence, for suffering, and for merit.
Most of the world will pass away.
And a good thing too. For it is largely a world
for which Saint John's Christ refused to pray.
Suffering in this view is a punishment for sin,
or a penance that precedes forgiveness and reward.

The objects of our pain and toil, the work we do
and suffer for, are of little or no moment
in themselves. The will, the intention
of the worker, is almost exclusively significant.

Other ramifications are legion, but the caricature should be clear—and it has its point. The problem here is not the denial of, but the failure effectively to *experience*,

the humanity of Christ
and the seriousness with which he took our history
and his own.
Salvation will be through suffering,
not *in* and through it.
It is a deficient humanism.
Some, but relatively few men, probably,
live their entire lives this way.
Considerably more, perhaps, live half their lives
this way. They build the world, as most men do,
taking their joys and sorrows as they come.
And on the side, they plan for heaven.
It is a blueprint for the divided man.
Yet in the mercy of God, it has given him saints.

A good pendulum swing from this position we find a second view of what salvation is, and when. The time

is now.
The humanity of God structures everything here,
along with our incorporation into Christ
at baptism. The lovely greek patristic idea
of the divinization of man is taken at its word,
and a humanism of noble and boundless energy
ensues.
The flesh of the historical Christ
is part of the world, and all creation shares
its splendor, or at least its possibilities.
The redemptive act of Christ is abroad
to full effect—a *realized* eschaton, with history
and time under the nearly absolute control
of the christic dynamism now possessed by man.
Baptism may even be subverted,
in the view that redemptive contact with the flesh
of Christ is an *effectively* and not just
potentially universal situation and quality,
rather than a specifically Christian thing,
however hidden.

At its apogee, this humanism bids fair
to compromise prayer, displacing rather more
than complementing it by the dialogue
of brotherhood.
Liturgy will focus on *one* of its several
great truths, on fellowship, with little place
for adoration. And why not, if every man
is God in Christ, or may be, in a sense that asks
for no *operatively* significant distinctions.

A discussion of extremes would lead us
to the Incarnation as permanent death of God,
and this trinitarian death would leave us
with one who is not that Son

whose very *manhood*

and delight lay in his Father's will.
With Peter, our eyes on Tabor would lift to find
the Jesus of history only:
a nobler, but finally not less defeated Socrates,
and not also the transfigured Christ
of our and Peter's *faith*.

The mysterious character of sin grows dim
in this humanism that we speak of here,
as man at least risks being circumscribed
as mere history or even as object
of the social sciences—albeit an object
of surpassing difficulty to analyze and master.
Suffering is an anomaly and a scandal
in this view of man. But it is not so divorced
from salvation as in the former view. For here,
optimism, and hope in the present
and in the immediate future, governs all.
Salvation is brotherhood
in a prosperous if often difficult
and challenging city of man (a much less ascetical
view than the former, but an equally non-mystical
one, of man before God in the world).
This salvation lies within the reach,
if not of this generation, then the next,
if only there be sufficient men free
and courageous enough to grow to their full stature.
Salvation here

is not the triumph of love over hate,
through suffering and death.
It is the destruction of suffering

by a free mankind that does not need,
or at least no longer needs, redemption.

This humanism takes both salvation and suffering
very seriously. But here the two
are not a mysterious, rhythmic paradox,

breeding lilacs out of the dead season.

They are antagonists.
Salvation lies not through,
but in the destruction of,

the cross.

Another caricature, it must emphatically be insisted, but also with its point—indeed with a very rudimentary and central point, for prayer.

The third view of salvation, as might have been expected, lies the middle way, but it is not less adventurous for that. It radically allows man's continuing dependence, for the profound divinization worked in him by baptism

remains sheer gift,
which is the indwelling not just of the spirit
and eclat of the historical Christ,
but of the Holy Spirit of the risen Lord,

who is in man and for him,
but not of him.

And again, it is the body of the one
historical and *risen* Christ
which the Father has made the cornerstone
of the now intrinsically valuable city of man.
And that is why the worker in this city,
whether he throws rivets or a baseball,
whether he cries out for joy because a child is born
or screams in suffering from cancer,
or lives with tough nobility
in the confines of neurosis
—this worker is doing something that need never die.
For if it is human, it may become a part of Christ.
In this view, the world is both
religious and profane,
and that's the way it should be.

But it is wholly christic.
It is an inaugurated eschaton, the biblical
theologians say.

There is a road to go, a passage to be made.

And it does lead beyond history,
to the risen Lord who draws all creation to himself,
to the honor of his Father,
who shall then be all in all.

And yet the paradox.
The acceptable time is *now,*
for the Kingdom of God is among us,

and the summer rains have begun to ripen
the April sowing.

The God-man's body glitters all about us.
In an often muddy epiphany, to be sure.
And the bulldozers do a work that's needed,
but a work that need not pass. (Of course
that is nonsense where there is no faith.)

Christ is alive,
and deeply in love with all mankind.
And men, some men,

have even now turned fond eyes on one
another.

And that's salvation:
the death of hate, and the birth in us
of the love of the Father for his only Son
and all Christ's scattered brothers.
Salvation has begun. Now.

But it is a difficult enterprise.
Hate is allowed to test the victory in us,
for human love takes time.
And the building blocks of our city
are recalcitrant and hard,
and ever awake to a humanism
that insists it is its own,
and not the gift of the humanity of its risen Lord.
Or conversely, their bruising recalcitrance
—or their awesome beauty—may invite us to believe
that there is nothing here worth doing,
except to be tempted and to wait.

For either temperament, the desperate nights
of faith seek idols for our tired eyes,
and we are once more urged to adore
our isolated selves.
This is our suffering, and we are diminished
by our struggle and our pain.
But the Christ in us grows great by it.

Our love of Christ, our fellow men,
and of our world, will be the death of us.
That is God's own truth, and our way to life.
Salvation—in and through suffering, loneliness,
and death.

It was a broken body in the tomb
that marked the moment and occasion

when a young man strode across the sunrise.

II
PRAYER: LIFE WITH GOD IN THE CITY OF MAN

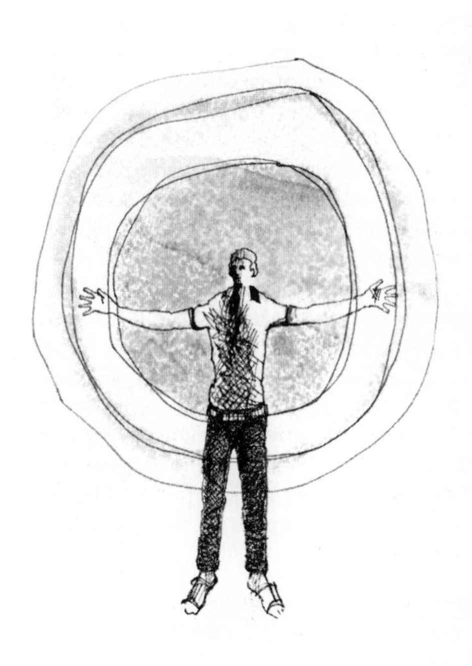

3. Prayer and Religion

A subject so rich as religion and prayer demands a modest reach. The attempt here will be just to say what religion and prayer are fundamentally about and to suggest that, at this fundamental level, religion and prayer—and man too—are one and the same act and event. In doing this, we will be using, to a very significant extent, the thought and vocabulary of the religious thinker and spiritual director, Friedrich von Hügel.[1] But before beginning, a few preliminary remarks.

First, the reader will not find here any discussion of such rightly tortured, directly pastoral questions as: how is secular and religious man to enact and dramatize his own complex reality, and what are the forms and styles, the places and the times for both corporate and individual prayer as suggested or required by contemporary psychology and sociology, or by the great signs and calls of the Spirit's peremptory judgment on our times: our wars, our racism and our neighbor's poverty. Such matters do and ought deeply to determine the very possibility as well as the shape of our religion and our prayer. We shall pray only in terms of them. But the view here is that none of them *are* religion and prayer. And our intention is basic: to say what religion and prayer are about. This suggests that it is possible—without thereby seeming disinterested—to transmit consideration of those social and political situations (be they joys, or sorrows, or sins) in which religion and prayer get their blood (or lose it), and in which they find their body. It also supposes that to be basic is not thereby automatically to be abstract. For example, if to be directly, nakedly trinitarian—as we are at moments—is to be difficult (and it is), it is, we hope, not to talk geometry. Perhaps it is primarily

> not our ideas, but our experience,
> not the state so much of our theology
> as of our spirituality,

that decides whether the Godhead as Trinity
is a notion we have,
or a complex life we greet, and do,
and become man by.

A second initial remark concerns the vast question of the language itself: religion and prayer. We cannot even begin to deal with it here. However, we can remind ourselves

that these words speak to mysteries and realities
which englobe us and in which we come to be;
that they come to us even as language
with rich histories of their own;
and that we do not so much assign their meanings
—much less pretend wholly to produce the realities
of which they speak—as welcome them
with the reverence due great gifts.

It is better, with humility, to set a word aside,
to let it rest a while in the silence
of its secrets (when we cannot read its promise),
than either tailor such a word to passing custom
and so defuse its power to reveal,
or 'clarify' it beyond its power to amaze.

At any rate von Hügel, and this essay as well, take religion and prayer as words still vibrant with the holy 'fact' and the human adventure they have quite traditionally named.

Our final opening remark concerns prayer. We want to give a preliminary description of it now, so that it will be ready to hand when we discuss prayer in the context of our subject, that is vis-à-vis religion.

When read with sympathy,
the old description does us very well:
prayer is the raising of the mind and heart to God.
'Attending' might do better than 'raising'.
And 'response' is more accurate yet.

For all prayer is response to the divine initiative:
He loved us first, as Saint John says.
And he spoke first too.
And he continues to speak.
He only says one Word—but it will do.
It is enough.
For the Word is Christ, who is everything
and the only thing the Father has to say.
Even petitionary prayer is a response.
For it is only in terms of promises made,
and that sheer fidelity which is the history
of God's action with Israel and the Church,
that we ask for anything at all as Christians.

So prayer is the response of the mind
and heart to God.

Of course mind and heart here must be grasped
as historical movement and flesh.
They mean the *whole* man, as he is:
spirit-in-a-*body*-in-the-*world;*
they mean man consciously and freely aware of God
from within and through the reality and situation
of man himself as personal, social, material
and changing.
But that prayer is primarily consciousness of *God*
and not of self, or world, or of brother either,
continues to hit the nail on the head.
This immediately excludes any least suggestion
(not unheard of) that prayer,
either in its whole reality, or in its substance,
is the middle term of some observe-reflect-and-act
life program.
That is not what prayer means.

Prayer is not reflection,
and it is not aimed at mental or emotional
hygiene or health—or at social concern
or action either.
Any more than human love is.
It is not aimed at self-help or conditioning.
It is not some pep-talk to myself,
that is, it is not *actually* a monologue
—though under some traditional
but really fictitious language of dialogue—
aimed at purifying and deepening
and bracing myself for fuller, nobler moral action.
Nor, finally, is it aimed at the constitution
of human, even ecclesial community.
Any more than love is.

Oh we may pray *for* these things,
and we may certainly hope to experience
these things as valued *by-products* of our prayer
and as paramount in *God's* intention
toward our prayer.

Now it is true that prayer is radically contextual.
And therefore it is emphatically the case
that the materials, events and persons
of our secular existence, that what we read or see,
that what we and our fellow men suffer and need
and laugh for joy at,
are the very materials and times of our prayer,
and that all these realities both affect

and get shaped by our prayer
and give to it its body and its history.
They are, and they do.

But they are not the heart of prayer's mystery.
God is.

And this is so, whether the prayer
be adoration, thanksgiving, petition or contrition.
Prayer is not aimed at anything at all.
Like love, which it is or hopes to be,
prayer is utterly for itself,
without remainder.

Though it *has* remainders—explosively so—
since personality, and community, and world
occur and come to be as gift of God
especially through prayer.

Romano Guardini expresses himself similarly
about liturgical prayer:
'It expresses itself by the absence of aim.
The liturgy does not wish to achieve *anything,*
but merely wants to dwell in the presence of God;
to breathe and unfold, to love and praise him.' [2]
This is well said. It makes the point so blatantly
that you have either to deal with it
or to walk away from it.
But you can't misunderstand it: The liturgy
does not wish to achieve *anything,*
but merely want to dwell in the presence of God.

Now of course, where this is *well done,*
there should be, once again, explosive results.
The *by-products* of all Christian prayer,
whether private prayer or liturgical prayer,
should be at once self-fulfillment
of the individual person, the *creation*
as well as the *expression* of community,
and vigorous social action.
And the presence or absence of these by-products,
these *God*-intended results of prayer,
are the sound criteria of all experimentation
and reform.
But where they are *aimed* at,
that is, where prayer is pragmatized,
then they destroy prayer,
and, of course, as genuine prayer's by-products,
they destroy themselves,

at least insofar as they are gifts God gives
through prayer.

Prayer is radically a *mis-en-presence*,
as the French writers on the subject put it:
a coming into God's presence, a *being taken*
into God's presence.
When we make petition to one another,
it is the one who is prayed to who is absent.
'I will go and see him.'
And so of our contemplation of one another too.
I want just to be with my friend whom I love.
'I will go and be with him.'
In our prayer to *God,*
it is *we* who are absent, not God.
Augustine says it splendidly: thou wast with me,
but I was not with thee.
We hear so much about the absence of God.
It needs careful consideration.
Perhaps it is man who is absent.
And we hear about the silent God.
Perhaps that Word which is Christ
is as extant and as proffered as ever,
and it is we who can't hear,
because we've lost the art of listening,
of just being there, of contemplating.
Prayer, then, at any rate, occurs in the presence
of God.

And God here is not a background for reflection
on our moral endeavor, however suitable.
Nor is he a value, or an idea,
or an ideal that we meditate about
—though all these things may profitably lead to
or flow from prayer.
God—the Christian God—is a person.
He is the Father of our Lord Jesus Christ.
Prayer, as Maurice Nédoncelle so forcefully puts it,
exists entirely in the realm of the vocative,[3]
that is, it is an encounter, a dialogue,
an interpersonal relationship
—whether with Lord and servant,
Savior and sinner,
or, as Ignatius of Loyola puts it so beautifully
as he echoes the book of Exodus:
a talking things over as friend with friend.

The presuppositions of prayer, then,

as understood here, seem clear:
the reality of a *personal God who speaks,*
and the possibility of *man's experiencing* this God.
And the experience itself, of course,
where *fully* itself, would be a reply,
a reply to the Father.
But it is always a reply to what he is saying.
So it is always a reply in Christ.
And the fact of faith is not just
that the Father *has spoken.*
He *is speaking.*

> For his Word endures,
> and his deed remains done.
> He continues to say and he continues to do
> that one Word and Deed which is flesh and history
> —as Christ, as Scripture, as Church,
> and as Eucharist.

Now in our human interpersonal relationships
—our communication in love with one another—
all sorts of things go on:
praise, thanksgiving, petition,
and the asking for pardon.
But these things, even between man and man,
always occur in function of something more prior:
the relationship itself
as something not pragmatic, not manipulated,
the relationship of love
as a value in and for itself.

My friend *is.*
And that is—wonderful.
A man's wife *is,*
and his personal presence to her,
his conscious and free *being with her,*
in and for herself;
his conscious and free affirmation of her value,
of her person

> *just because she is*

—quite prior to what he may do for her
or what she may do for him (and indeed as *condition*
of those by-products and effects
being fully human and holy)—
well, this is love, which has no reasons

or purposes—which is its own reason.
And it is love—which is the point here—

coming to be and acting itself out
as contemplation:

that turning toward the other,
that alert, self-surrendering personal presence
to the other in *their* mystery and joy and wonder
—just because they are,
because they are there,

because they are so.

This is not easy, of course,
but rather involves a great effort and death
to self—at least if love has a faithfulness
and is not a mere moving from one infatuation
or romance to another.
Fidelity at this level and of this quality,
whether in friendship, marriage or prayer,
—that wonderful word fidelity—
is a severe and costly thing.

Fidelity is one of God's words,
one of the great words for God's love.
And we know what it cost him.
It cost him Christ.

Now this turning to God,
this conscious and free presence of two freedoms
to one another in interpersonal relationship,
is the heart of prayer. It is contemplation,
in a quite basic, childlike, indispensable sense.
This is what prayer is.
And while prayer's *situations,*
and maybe its techniques too, can and do
and should radically differ—from time to time
and from person to person—and while prayer's
results too should radically differ
precisely because its situations
and the persons involved so radically differ,
yet there seems nevertheless nothing
at once fundamental *and* fashionable to say
about some special prayer suitable to the 1970s.

'Thy kingdom come, thy will be done,
give us this day our daily bread.'

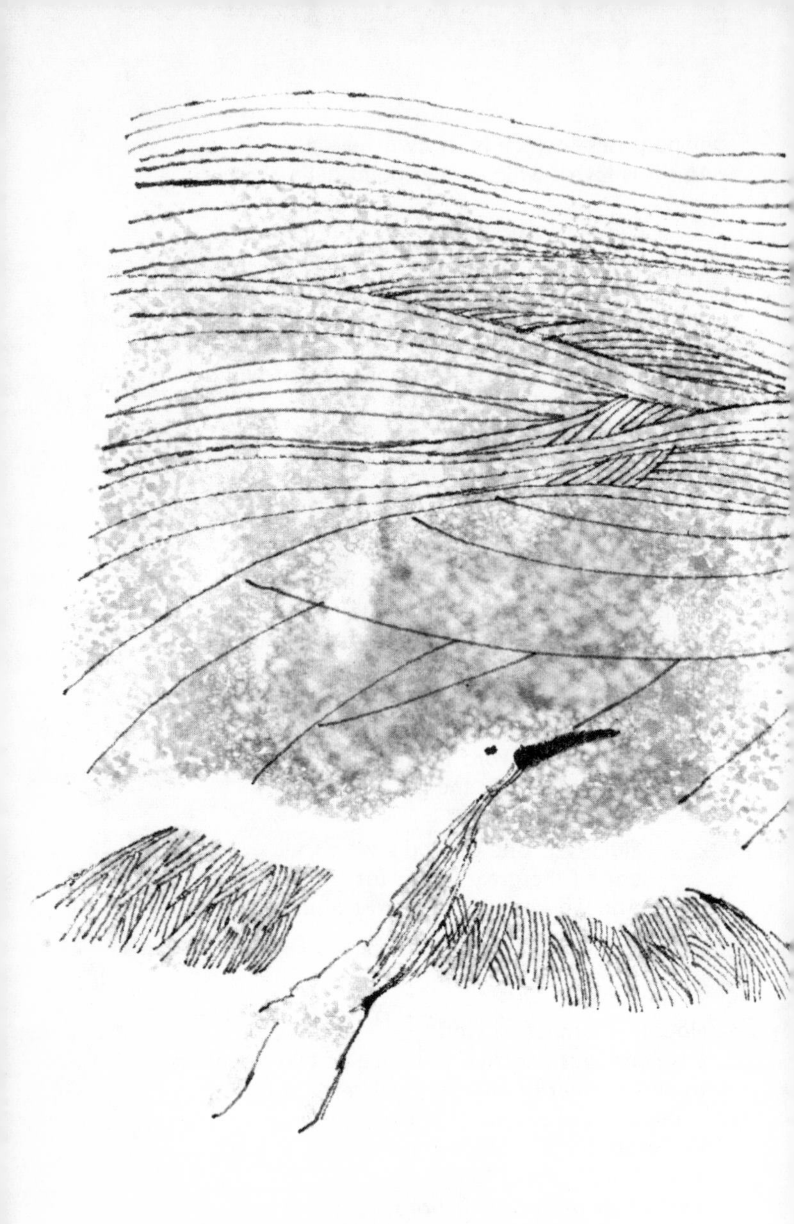

These petitions are both radically the same
and radically unique for every man and culture
that prays them well.
But there is something prior to them all:

our Father:
the Father of our Lord Jesus Christ:

the Father of John and Paul, of Augustine
and Teresa,
and of all our brothers and sisters
in the contemporary people of God.

Prayer is conscious and free presence
to this Father.
Prayer is radically contemplation.

Further on, we shall also be looking to see how the substance of mysticism and ecstasy (not their famous or infamous phenomena) name the being of prayer. We turn now, however, to present (with a good deal of editorializing of our own) von Hügel's thought on our subject of prayer and religion.

Religion is the 'deepest of all experiences
of the deepest of all facts'.

This is the central statement, and the effort will be to show that it is also a definition of prayer as who and what man fundamentally is. Several things are immediately in view. First,

if religion is the experience of a fact,
then religion is, in its own interiority,
twofold:

it is the Fact of God,
and it is man's experience of that fact.

Second, if religion is man's *deepest*
experience of God,
then there are other possible experiences of him.
But we prescind from this consideration
at once (though it has importance),
since man as *religious* experience
alone concerns us here.

Third, if religion is the deepest experience
of the deepest of facts,
then there are *other* facts and other experiences:
religion is not pietism.

'However much man may be supremely and finally a religious animal, he is not *only* that; but he is a physical and sexual, a fighting and an artistic, a domestic and social, a political and philosophical animal as well.'

Secularity is in full view here,
and a good thing for religion too.

For only a mankind and a world
given the space and time, and allowed the autonomy
and interiority required to be and to become
—just simply themselves—

only such a mankind and world
can be and do the suitably rich praise of God.

The point is that neither secularism
nor pietism will do.
Man is both secular and religious,
at once and to the end. Dualism, then,
but no dichotomy. Real distinction,
but without separation (like God in his Trinity).

Man is an organism,

and his destined simplicity is never
an 'empty oneness'. He is a *'harmony'*,
given as gift and accomplished as task
through the conflicts and tensions, the cross
and the peace, the rhythmic involvements
and detachments of concrete and historical,
both sinful and redeemed, existence.

Too quickly to 'solve' man
is to reduce his wager and promise,
generally in one of two ways:
either by a secularism
which remands him and his world
wholly into the custody of himself (who
can survive self-love?),
or by a pietism
which leaves him a bloodless shadow on the earth.

The old, central mystery of spirituality
remains pressed:
man comes to himself as man
only in and through 'this wonderful world'
and the 'good things of this life'.
Yet 'how much leisure and pay is the miner
to have, till he is to be helped to love prayer
and the thought of God?'

But we are jumping ahead, and exceeding our subject.

Religion—to take up our point—
is a fact and an experience.

It is a divine fact and a human event.
It is the sheer fact of God,
and what happens to man, that fact, i.e. God,
being so. It is dialogal, then, and has existence
only as relationship.

As *including* God in himself, it is clear that religion cannot be subject to any systematic criticism as idolatry, nor can Christianity be had without remainder as religionless.[4] Yet as also including *man's* experience, religion is the proper subject of continual purification, growth and change, and human freedom is a condition of its very existence.

But it is of course religion, and not God (and therefore religion only partially), which is so dependent on man. Here we want to press our reference to God as Fact and make our meaning very clear, indeed blatant.

> Though religion cannot even be conceived as extant at all without a human subject humanly apprehending the Object of religion, the Reality of the Object (in itself the Subject of all subjects) and its presence independently of all our apprenhension of it . . . its *Givenness,* is the central characteristic of all religion worthy of the name. The Otherness of God, the onesided relation between God and man, these constitute the deepest measure and touchstone of all religion.

The *basic* structure of religion, then,
is not suffering and desire, but

the 'Joy of God'

taken as that utter, and utterly successfully
accomplished and being accomplished: giving,
receiving, and having; that utter
being-toward-the-Other of Father and of Son
as lover and beloved—which is Spirit;
and all this as 'Given' and 'There',
as 'Overagainst' and prior to man.

Suffering and desire are religious too.
They name *man* in his sinful being
and his historical becoming.

They structure man's journey into God's joy.
Not that man's joy is altogether future,
or in no way his own.
No, joy is the world too, now that the Spirit
is given.

But the Fact of God
is profoundly *history* as *Cross,*
and thus it is that our joy
so often has the figure of a restlessness
that conceals his lovely advance.

This 'fact of God' can certainly fail of encounter; it can certainly be denied and rejected too. Von Hügel's point here is simply that this is what religion is:

> Try and prove, if you will, that religion is untrue; but do not mislead yourself and others as to what constitutes its power and its worth.

And again:

> The experiences of religion always present their object as overflowingly existent . . . as perfect Self-conscious Spirit, as very source of all existence and reality. We can indeed argue against religion as mistaken in so doing; but that religion actually does so, and this, not in the form of deductive reasoning, but in that of intuitive experience, cannot seriously be denied.

'Experience':
this completes our description of religion,
and it takes us closer to religion both as prayer
and as 'characteristic' of man,
that is, as making him what and who
he fundamentally is.
Experience here is the conscious and free
and emotional, that is, human,
appropriation of what is *given* and *there*
as *offered* to conscious freedom:
the fact of God.

There is a dialectic here, descriptive of man's
very being.
For while experience does not make, or construct,
or grasp this God (he is 'simply given,

not sought and found'),
yet he is there only as offered
to freedom ('God himself is apprehended
only if there be action of our own').
And *man* is given—he occurs and comes to be
as man (it is a journey)—
only in the freedom (itself a gift)
by which he welcomes God.
This is man as religious experience.

It is also prayer,
and it suggests that man is prayer.
For prayer is the attending of the whole man to God.
It is the welcomed 'penetration of spirit by Spirit',
mediated and expressed (without magic or mechanics)
by and through man's mind and emotions and body,
through history and things,
through effort and training and habits and tears,
and by inter-action with and for
the brother in community.
It is *history,* therefore, an incarnational
and worldly event.

> But it is nevertheless a *direct and immediate*
> meeting with and a wholly personal invasion by
> God himself in his Trinity.

Now if we stay with their substance,
this is what mysticism is, and ecstasy too.
They name man's being as prayer.
And *given* the fact and gift of God,
mysticism and ecstasy are what we may expect to do
and to have happen:
they pertain to the *'normal* consciousness of
mankind'.[5]

For mysticism is the 'experience (more or less
clear and vivid)
of God as distinct, self-conscious Spirit',
'the emotional apprehension of the already full
operative existence of eternal beauty, truth,
goodness, of infinite Personality and Spirit,
and this independently of our action'.

But this is nothing but religion,
the heart of it as prayer.
And as consciousness of *God,* it is ecstasy too

—which raises the whole question
of 'active' and 'passive'. Of course,
the first truth of the whole matter is gift:

it is *God's* love which revolutionizes man

and brings him continually into both
terrible crisis and harmonious growth.
But the term passivity tells this truth
at considerable risk and cost.

For who has ever been successfully loved,
except through his own freedom and action
as well?

Experience and prayer are love,
or they are nothing at all. And for man
as well as for God, while experience and prayer
are *never* 'activity' or activism (a busy,
distracted and distracting milling about,
with the self and *its* plans and powers
always in view),
they nevertheless have their whole being as *'action':*
the moving out into the Gift, into the love
and the lover, by which we become ourselves
(as do Father and Son for each other,
and as does man before God in prayer).

This is ecstasy,
and there is nothing odd whatever about it
—though of course there is everything extraordinary.
But that is because it is love,
which is always a wonder:

the moving out
into and for the sake of the others and Other,
by which man comes to be as man.

It is a mighty deed and an explosive event,
this accepting of great gifts,
as Mary of Nazareth discovered.
Where well done, there is ardent ease:
that total involvement with the other
without thought of self and at whatever cost to self
which we call enthusiasm.
There is nothing frantic here, but only gentleness,
and the largely unremarked if terribly painful
death of selfishness.

It is ecstasy: the loss, not of consciousness,
but of self-consciousness; the abeyance,
not of choice, but of the choice of self.
In prayer, it is the utter preoccupation with God,
from which simply *has* to occur

a total preoccupation with all that God loves:

a world,
and a world of men.

Mysticism and ecstasy as prayer
are freedom,
the event we dream of,
the adventure man was born for
and the grace he is:

to be a man.

Von Hügel's man is prayer then,
and his thought suggests we shall find out
at judgment

that the story of man's prayer
is the significant history of the world.

For *man is what happens*
when fleshed spirit
is well met by and greets God in history.

The paradox persists:
if religion and prayer are the fact and gift of God,
they are nevertheless a human event.
And yet this human event which is man
will *fully* occur only as prayer,
as immediate encounter with God.
Von Hügel's man is a journey
from the isolated self into community;
the forced march (it is not easy)
from the impoverishment of self-occupation
(whether an individual's or a culture's)
into dialogue with the brother, the world
and with God;
a movement from the animal self, however clever
or sophisticated,

into personality.

As prayer,
personality is the conscious free-willing spirit
organized for self-surrender
through invasion by the Trinity.
Saint John assures us:
it is *both* Father and Son who 'come'.[6]
Man in the Spirit is the *historical* grace and freedom
of *both* the Father's love of the Son
and the Son's love of the Father.
He is the *secular* movement
wherein the larger, the total Son,
fleshed for history as Christ and world
and world of men,
gets declared and effected.
And he is the *religious* movement and cry:
'Abba, Father!'

Here we glimpse the broader issue, far broader than the subject of this essay. But it is the broader issue for *prayer* too.

For if prayer as immediate encounter with God
is always in itself religious,
it is nevertheless *in* prayer (because in the Spirit)
that man gets declared as secular
and continually discovers the shape and extent
of his mission in the world.

This invites lengthy, precise development—but not in this essay where we are looking at the specifically *religious* experience of man as prayer.

The basic structure of this religious experience as prayer and of prayer as man seems to be marian:

let it happen to me according to your word.

This woman provokes and enters upon
her whole history as Mary
and arrives in triumph upon herself as human
through the humility of a creaturely but free
and conscious welcome to and appropriation of
the Fact of God as Other and as Gift.
Precisely as prayer, therefore,
she is the archetypal Christian and fitting image
of the Church:

let it happen to me.

Let it (the real, what is
and in the first place, He Who Is)
be, be so, let him and all that's real, occur.

Let (as an active, creative, 'costly',
free-willing and personal appropriation,
an ardent letting be),
let the entire real, finally personal,
initially and ultimately Personal,

happen to me.

The whole effort and argument here
begins and ends with the *religious* experience
of man in the world
as that historical and evolutionary gift
of God's very own self,
which in prayer come to be man's own self too
in his destiny as graced and free reply to God:

hallowed be thy name:
let God be God.

Fundamentally then, man as personality
is prayer as adoration.
Maurice Nédoncelle therefore can rightly say
that for von Hügel, human personality

'is the final goal of the world,
for which even the heavens wait'.

And prayer as petition finally and at the last
is nothing but a request
that man may become and do this adoration:
thy will be done (Jesus in the garden,
as well as Mary before God as newly proposed
Incarnate Fact: let it happen to me).
Petition is profoundly a program of struggle
and purification. Deeply undertaken,
it asks for the shattering of idols,
that man may be adoration.

Let God be God: therefore,
let only *God* be God.

And it is here perhaps that precisely religious man
as prayer requests and wills his secularity.
For only a vigorous purity in worship,
theology and ecclesiastical polity

allows man to emerge as man and lets the world
be world: autonomous and with their own interiority.
A valid man and a robust world,
and not their shadows or stunted distortions,
are the truth. And

> if only the real God is to be adored,
> only a real man can adore him.

If it is in function of himself as freely,
consciously appropriated trinitarian image and gift
that man is love of both God and world,
then of course only religious man,
the man who prays, can fully manage the terrors
and accomplish the joys of his destiny
as thorough secularity.
But it nevertheless remains for this secular destiny
to be managed and accomplished, if man is to be man.
And this imperatively suggests that

> only man come to prayer
> with a deeply worldly heart
> is the full adoration of God.

By way of conclusion now, we may briefly
acknowledge just a few implications and questions
in connection with what has been said.

1. Religion is not ethics. If prayer as religion is
primarily man before the 'Is-ness' of God, then only
in and through and because of this does ethics
('ought-ness') occur

> as the journey man must take
> to do and become personality,
> that God may become what he is:
>
> God *for man*.

2. If the whole position seems to suggest that
prayer is an incarnational preoccupation with
*dis*carnate transcendence, with God the Father
(through Christ and the world and in community),
and that this preoccupation is direct, immediate and
personal, then the position has been understood.
Von Hügel's christocentrism is

an experience of brotherhood as *son*ship in the Son,
and any untrinitarian christocentrism
thus becomes for him a *cul-de sac,*
where Christ is the last, most subtle idol of all
and our most plausible (because splendidly humanist)
escape from man's individual and corporate destiny,
which is

the love, in Christ, of *God* in Christ.

3. The position may seem a veritable climbing of the mountain of God—a risky proposal to modern

city-dwellers. Von Hügel cheerfully pleads guilty here. But the incarnational character of his theocentrism provides a counter to the charge that the climb is too steep or the air too rare and unworldly. Von Hügel's God comes 'all the way down' to man in Christ. Two points are made here, and both are stressed:

God *comes,*
and it is *God* who comes.

And man as reply receives his structure from God's deed:

he is a reply to God in *Christ,*
and to *God* in Christ.

There is the question of strain, of course, in the light of changing patterns of culture, nerves and occupations. But the very necessary moderation of modern man must not lack great ambition (under grace), 'unless, indeed, Dante is to disappear before Tennyson, and Beethoven before Sir Arthur Sullivan'.

4. There are the further huge and practical questions of *how* a man should pray (corporate, vocal, mental, 'formless'), and of how *much* a man (and different groups in the community) should pray, and when, and where. A developed answer would fight shy of generalizations. Yet to say that

prayer must occur
if the undiluted human adventure of man as person
is to take place at all,

is to say that prayer too, like everything human, must have its times. And there is imperative usefulness in asking, carefully, after its places and its gestures as well

—at least if man as history,
as spatial-temporal enactment of spirit,
is taken seriously.
Surely we know enough about human love for this.
And if prayer is always more than human love,
it is not only never less,
but it is always human too.

5. Another question concerns why prayer should be

so difficult (and it is, even when loved), if prayer is what man is. We cannot delay here, but we may ask at once:

who would suppose, in our time, that it is easy,
or even that it takes only moderate effort,

to be a man?

Sin and concupiscence
(as both individual and cultural self-centeredness)
come however unfashionably to mind here.
So do humility and 'creatureliness . . .
the first term of every genuine spirituality'.

And really,

we sufficiently know
the problems we have and the purification needed
in assisting, and not manipulating or dominating
—in 'letting' the world be
and come to itself as world
and in letting our friends, and strangers too,
come to themselves precisely as other than us
and with their own reverenced autonomy
and interiority—
we surely know the difficulty of all this too well
to be surprised at the effort (itself a gift)
we must manage

if we are to welcome God as God.

And then too there is the difficulty
that God in Christ is not found or given
except in the world and through our fellow men.
There can be little impulse for prayer
—it is scarcely possible, in fact—
where there is no brotherhood, or where hunger
or racism inhibits and crushes
man's effective freedom and time
to assume his vocation as self-surrender.

We need to stay with and lengthily explore both the secular presuppositions of man as religious and the means and materials of his incarnational becoming as person. Yet the old question has to stay pressed while we do this: 'How much leisure and pay is the miner to have, till he is to be helped to love prayer and the thought of God?' And there is a similar question for those rightly busy in seeking the miner's justice.

6. Finally, it may also be asked about religion and prayer as man before the 'Is-ness' and 'Fact' of God: is not this a static situation, with little or no place for history, or for really significant novelty and surprise? And yet,

> nothing seems more eventful than
> man's worldly exploration into
> God's Joy.
>
> The Joy is certainly not static.
> For what is *there* as Fact, as Given, as Gift,
> is totally dynamic Act, ever at crest and new:
> the love affair of Father and of Son.
> And if this happens for itself *eternally,*
> it happens for *history,* for man,
> through the 'Yes:
>
> let it happen to me'
>
> of human freedom alone.
> Only then does what is Fact
> become personal and revolutionary *Presence*
> and salvation *History,*
>
> in which the individual comes to be as person
> and begins to be son and brother,
>
> and in which world comes to be as world
> and begins to be Kingdom of God.
>
> No, man and his world are not static either.
>
> > Man is an adventure that happens
> > when fleshed spirit consciously meets God
> > in the world
> > and greets him with the freedom of love.

This is our definition of prayer, and it is what we have meant by religion.

Von Hügel is well aware that his view of religion and prayer

> has not, for the more strenuous of our educated contemporaries, become . . . a living question at all. A morally good and pure, a socially useful and active life—all this in the sense and with the range attributed to these terms by ordinary parlance: this and this alone is, for doubtless the predominant public present-day consciousness, the true object, end, and measure of all healthy religion; whatsoever is alongside of, or beyond, or other than, or anything but a direct and exclusive incentive to this, is so much superstition and fanaticism.

We have not been especially concerned here to dispute this perhaps still current and moralistic, that is, exclusively ethical view of man. Not that there are 'proofs', anyway. It is a matter for experience, tested and discerned. The intention has rather been

simply to wonder
if the difficult nobility of this ethic
does not have its deeper ground
and its fuller possibility
in religion and prayer
taken as man at a still more primary level
of his career both as process and as gift:

I mean his direct experience of,
his conscious and free attention and response
of mind and heart to,

that 'Fact and Joy'
who is the God and Father
of our Lord Jesus Christ.

4. Contemplating Christ

The one mysterious reality which is prayer may be asked about from many points of view. In this essay—on contemplating Christ—we are at once in the quite specific area of Christian prayer and, even more exactly and concretely, we are concerned with the prayer of a Christian.

There is no quarrel among historians and theologians of prayer but that prayer is the central reality and act of all religion.[1] Christianity is a *religion*. However, Christianity is also, and with no less importance, an *historical* religion,

> a religion which comes into existence
> and has its shape
> from a God who speaks and acts in history.

As *religious* and not merely psychological or humanist, therefore, the prayer of a Christian will affirm the mystical—in the broad but strongly realist sense of a direct and immediate presence to, and invasion by, the utterly objective and wholly personal reality of a free and infinite God.[2] When prayer as the central and essential *religious* act is completely itself, therefore, it exists entirely in 'the realm of the vocative'. It speaks to 'a sphere of interpersonal relations in the solicitation of two liberties'.[3]

And as a specifically *Christian* religious act, this prayer of a Christian will affirm

> the absolutely divine
> and therefore definitive character
> of that quite precise, particular and definite,
> human *history* which is Jesus of Nazareth
> both in himself and in his, the Son's,
> continuing, developing incarnation
> as the one fleshed word and deed of his Father:
> scripture, eucharist, and that community
> of his body: the Church, his Father's sons.

Our title itself—contemplating Christ—is therefore ambiguous, and properly so. For it suggests an historical subject-matter (the life, death and example of Jesus of Nazareth)

at the same time that it affirms a presence to, and an interpersonal communication with, a divine Person (the present, eternal, quite objective reality of Jesus as victoriously risen Lord and Christ).

And whatever the difficulties involved, any theoretical view—whether exegetical, theological or pragmatic—which would effectively object to, and any actual *experience* which would significantly neglect or fail to encounter, either or both of these undoubtedly distinct but wholly inseparable and factual aspects of the matter, would be outside our declared subject of Christian prayer taken as the contemplation of Christ.

Further, and not as an alternative, but as a real addition to and penetration of the twofold consideration we have made, our title leaves itself open to a third, still more fundamental understanding and experience of Christian prayer,

> where 'contemplating Christ'
> speaks not only and not finally,
> either to a consideration of the historical
> mysteries of the life of Jesus of Nazareth,
> or (in and through such consideration) to a mystical,
> responding encounter with the risen Lord of history.
>
> But our title also speaks
> (and in and through both these two concrete
> encounters: therefore incarnationally
> and as an always christologically structured
> theocentrism)
> to a direct and immediate experience
> of the *God* of Jesus of Nazareth's
> and the risen Christ's *own* contemplative prayer:
>
> > the Father.
> > *His* Father, the Father of Jesus Christ.
>
> We are not sidestepping Jesus, therefore,
> in our insistence on this point.
> Rather we are merely penetrating to the central
> reality and mission of Jesus
> —and of ourselves too in our present,
> and not merely future, situation as adopted sons—
> his mission as revelation of,
> and ours as response to,
> the Father.

For Christ's whole reality, as Son, as man,
as scripture and as eucharist
—and the Christian's whole reality also,
insofar as he is a Christian,
that is, has his entire existence
as a new creation in Christ—
is from and toward the Father.

It will be our point to develop this situation of Christianity as preoccupation with the Father in our movement now to describe the two terms of our subject: contemplating Christ.

Contemplation, for an essay as basic as this, will have a broad, hopefully quite definite, but no very technical meaning. It will not be our purpose at all, therefore, to distinguish contemplation from meditation, vocal prayer, corporate worship, etc. in any precise way. Further, our treatment here will not speak to many other quite legitimate questions that concern both the history of contemplative prayer and that more immediately interesting reality which is the individual histories of men who contemplate: the stages of prayer; whether and when prayer is acquired, infused; the problem of ligature, etc.

In by-passing such questions, however, it is perhaps useful to be clear that where vocal prayer, liturgy, etc. are not at least incipiently and, at moments quite formally, also contemplative, they are not prayer at all. For to our mind, contemplation —in the sense intended here—is but the explicitation, the development and the driving home of what is primary and what is radically essential as at least minimally present in *all* prayer that is itself, that is, authentic, at all.

All prayer is the attending of the mind and heart
to God. If it is to be Christian prayer,
this response will be massively qualified,
of course, as a response to God *in Christ.*
At the moment, however,
it is to prayer as *response* that we are looking,
and we are wholeheartedly assuming
the several religious presuppositions
of this radically interpersonal situation:

1. The utter priority of God as gracious freedom:
he loves us first,
and that love remains primary
and altogether initiating
throughout the conversation and those
perhaps further, speechless unions
which may existentialize themselves
as contemplative prayer.

2. The divine love and freedom
as creative of truly *other* loves and freedoms.
God gives himself to man the contemplative
insofar as he gives to the contemplative
a truly free and really other—*self*.
Gift is the fundamental truth, of course.
All is grace.
But the gift is so totally given
that man's truly autonomous freedom
and deeply significant capacity for loving response
occurs increasingly, indeed in direct proportion
to the presence and self-donation
of the God of grace.

(We may find this situation
humbly yet nobly verified and shadowed
in our best love of one another
—as in successful friendship and marriage:
in that loss of self in the other
which constitutes our true coming to self
in and through the other,
that receiving of ourselves from another,
which is not infatuation, surely,
but the austere, responsible integrity
of human love.[4]
Our human loves are the shadows,
and they may even be the sacraments,
of contemplation.
The inner-trinitarian love of Father and of Son
—where the gift of self is so total
and the receiving of the other so unimpaired
that it constitutes the entire reality of the Lovers—
is the analogue and the destiny of both.)

Contemplation as a term attempts to seize
upon this naked, primary reality of man
as personal receptivity and *response,*
as a conscious and free, as a human *yes* to God.
In its purity as a term, it in no way rejects

or precludes, rather it transmits consideration of,
the materials, vehicles and gestures
of its own communication
—be they vocal or interior words,
scenes of Christ's life,

> or the daily round
> of the contemplative's fidelity or apostasy
> toward his brother.

To emphasize further, this response which is
prayer, is the response of a *man*.
Prayer as the attending of the mind and heart
is therefore the whole man—*fleshed* spirit
in the *world,*
with intellect and will and imagination
and emotions ruthlessly, joyfully, painfully
collected [5] (through whatever mortification,
organization, simplification, *death*
of the petty and scattered self may be required)

> —collected in arduous freedom
> for that meeting in the still-point of spirit
> where the Lover waits,
>
> whether in thunder, whisper, or in silence.

Where such contemplation presses toward itself
as wholly realized, actualized, there will occur
what may usefully be called ecstasy,
if that term can be soberly understood:
as that loss, not of consciousness,
but of the consciousness of self;
and that total abeyance, not of choice,
but of the choice of self.[6]

Here contemplation opens up on that union
which pauline mysticism knows
as transformation into Christ,[7]
and which the whole mystical tradition
struggles to formulate, without pantheism,
as an encountering of God 'without intermediary',
'without modes'—where the contemplative
'becomes one spirit with God'.[8]
Where orthodox and valid, this will emerge,
not in the loss of personality,
but rather in that terrifying and holy experience
of the self and of the world

evaluated entirely fom *God's* point of view.

> The contemplative becomes aware of himself
> at this point
> only as known through and through by God.
>
> He views the world now, himself,
> and his brothers—and he loves them—
> as they are known and loved by God.

There will be no solipsism,
but rather a detachment from and a zeal for man
and the world which may well look fanatic
to the man who does not pray well
or who does not pray at all.
For the apostolic action of the contemplative
will increasingly have the direct, uninhibited
and notably unfashionable quality
of the creating, redeeming God himself.

The terrible purity of God's holiness and truth
may well make a desert of terror and absence
at this juncture. Or again,
whether rhythmically or concomitantly with this,
the divine love may fashion of the contemplative
and his world a silent and hidden transfiguration.

Finally (in so brief a sketch
of an unplumbable adventure and mystery),
seeing all creation and himself *through* God,
the Christian contemplative discovers here *in* God
his own and the world's total identity in Christ,
whom alone the Father knows and loves.[9]

Such contemplation is a journey,
and this journey into God, or—more properly—
this invasion by him, will be no matter
of a magic moment.
Contemplative prayer is a *history*
that must recapitulate and existentialize (give
a new historical existence to)
both the destructive and the creative dynamisms
of Exodus, Sinai, Babylon and, pre-eminently,
the Lord's own and our baptismal plunge
into his pasch:
that long march of Israel as harlot and bride,[10]
and the journey of Jesus as bridegroom, scapegoat
and servant

—to Jerusalem and *the Father,*
through death and resurrection.

What is being suggested here
is that, for a Christian,
contemplative grace (encounter with the Father),
has a most specific and definite,
indeed a scandalously precise, structure.[11]
It has the structure
of the *history* of a *particular* nation
and, especially and primordially,
the structure of the *particular* jew
who was Jesus of Nazareth
and who is now the risen Lord of glory:

the *slain* Lamb who *stands.*[12]

Contemplative grace is the grace of Christ.
For God has visited his people,
speaking through his prophets and his own
saving acts.
And in these last, quite definitive times
he has personally and as *Word*
taken flesh as Jesus of Nazareth,
and *that* Word forever now in victory
stands as slain:

fleshed forever with,
and Lord precisely in terms of,
all the details of his history.[13]

Contemplation is communion in love with the Father.
But from all eternity,
through the days of his flesh, until now,
this Jesus is the one Word of this God the Father.
Christ is everything and the only thing
the Father has to say.

Contemplative prayer, therefore, as response to, as
union with, as transformation into, the loving, that
is, proffered reality of the Father, formally brings
us to the second term of our one subject:

contemplating *Christ.*

Contemplative prayer
has singly to do with man's human response,
his conscious and free saying yes, to the love of God.

Within a Christian and social, thoroughly apostolic
perspective, this existential *yes*
with one's whole person and history
—which is what contemplative prayer wants to be—
will become an 'adhesion to the saving design
of God': [14]
that pauline *mysterion* [15] and lukan salvation history
which, especially in the johannine theology,
is *revealed* to be the Person of the Word,
Jesus Christ himself.

For the Christian, then,
who believes that God has revealed himself
in the particular history of Jesus,
contemplation of God is, without remainder,
contemplation of Christ.

However, as we said earlier, this contemplation of Christ may be viewed in at least three ways:

it may signify the contemplation of the historical life and death of Jesus as presented in scripture;

or it may point to that contemplation which is personal presence to and communication with the risen Christ now reigning with his Father as first fruit of the eschatological kingdom;

or it may suggest a contemplation and service of the God beyond the world and beyond the humanity of Christ too—Christ's Father—a contemplation which may be thought to structure Christ's own historical prayerful existence and which, for us, would occur only *in and through* the humanity of Christ.[16]

For many—and among them are serious modern men of prayer—the contemplation of Christ in the gospels raises some difficulty. Perhaps the central problem for some concerns the historical character of the portraits of Christ—a problem stimulated by the modern, quite legitimate criticism of scripture as a human, cultural document.[17] This criticism has discovered at least three strata in our gospels:

1. The actual life and actual words of the historical Jesus (*Sitz im Leben Jesu*);

2. This life and those words as reflected and formulated in the experience and the needs of

the early Christian community—a community founded upon its *easter,* that is, resurrection faith in Jesus and upon pentecost (*Sitz im Leben der Kirche*);

3. Finally, the level of the gospel itself as the literary document we now have, wherein a single evangelist, or a school, selects, interprets and organizes the material of the previous two levels from a particular perspective or theological point of view (*Sitz im Evangelium*).

For the Christian as exegete and scientific historian, a whole range of problems is in view here. And for the Christian *as a man coming to prayer,* the solution of some of these problems is of immense advantage.

For the more deeply and accurately he grasps the dynamisms, content and intentions of this organic event and word which is the gospel, and the more fully he understands the inter-action especially between the first two levels and the third, the more exactly will he know and be able to *hear* (and therefore properly *respond* to) what is being said to him on this third level, that is,

> the gospel of God which is Christ
> as he is now being proclaimed to us
> in the preaching community of the Church.

But for the Christian man of faith as *contemplative*—that is, not as *coming* to prayer, but as precisely and formally *man of prayer*—

> it is only this last, this third level,
> which is of concern.
> At this level only are the gospels a prayer-book
> in which one listens and replies
> to the self-revealing God
> speaking and acting in history.
> For it is at this level only that the gospels
> are inspired, are *word of God*
> in a quite serious sense (through that furthest
> kenosis of the eternal Word,
> humbling himself to flesh as Jesus
> and, here, to the written syllable as Scripture).[18]
> Here God the Father directly confronts man,
> through the instrumentality and sacramentality
> at once of Jesus, of the faith

of the easter community,
and of the psychology and theology of the evangelist.

And so the Christian contemplative
contemplates the gospel on his knees,

in adoration and unconditional obedience.

There is a second difficulty connected with the Christian's contemplation of the gospel text, a difficulty which arises from the fact that

all contemplative prayer (as we have seen now)
moves to, and is not completely itself except as,
an interpersonal relationship
between two liberties present to one another.
Christian contemplative prayer, then,
is union with the living, risen Lord,
actively present *now*
as Master and Servant of contemporary history.
He is not a child, he does not suffer or die
or walk the roads of Galilee,
and he never will again.

What has the past enshrined in the gospels to do with the living relationship of contemplation?

Yet just who *is* this victoriously risen Lord
the Christian contemplates?
The 'risen' alone reminds us of his history
and recalls to us all the details
—especially the death—of his flesh.
He is, as we saw,
'the Lamb standing as though slain'.[19]
The eternal Christ is not just the *product*
or the *aftermath* of his thirty years at Nazareth
and his paschal adventure into God.
He *is* this history, now.
Just as he was God as Jesus of Nazareth,
so now he has all the particularity and density
of this Jesus
in his present existence as Lord and Christ.
Indeed he is eternally constituted Lord and Christ[20]
by his Father
precisely in terms of his human history.

He is one 'Jesus Christ,

yesterday and today the same—and so forever'.[21]

Therefore the contemplation of the Jesus
of the gospels
is not an act of imagination
—in the sense of the construction of a fiction,
of someone who never existed,
or who no longer exists, in his earthly states
(as would be the case with Socrates).
These earthly mysteries of Jesus of Nazareth
exist *now* in the risen Lord.
They have achieved a new existence
and contemporaneity in his resurrection,
he who is now Master of history.
The literary documents which are the gospels
—if and where taken with utter seriousness
as word of God—
are thus the Father revealing to me
who his Son is *today*.

Such contemplative, that is, *experienced,* faith
enables the Christian man of prayer
radically to hope in history
(especially the novel segment of it
that is his own).
For it existentially notifies the contemplative
of his association in the paschal mystery of Christ
through his *own* passion, death and resurrection.
Some contemplation is absolutely essential,
therefore, if Christian man is to appropriate
and assist in his own redemption and humanization
—which he must do, if his redemption,
his holiness, his humanity,
are to be personal at all (that is, conscious
and free).

Where such contemplation of Jesus
presses to its mystical splendor
as transformation of the Christian into Christ
and of Christ into the Christian,[22]
exciting possibilities occur both for life
and for theology.

Hans Urs von Balthasar makes the point:

> Though objective revelation was concluded with the death of the last apostle, it does not

follow that, in the Church of saints, nothing further happens that touches on revelation. After all, the miracles of absolution and the consecration are continually repeated, and they bring about, again and again, a new presence of the events of Good Friday and Easter within the Church. Why should it not be the same with the constant repetition of the . . . *existence of the Lord* in the *life* (that is, not just in the doctrine, but in the actual dark night and the joys) of his faithful and saints? [23]

And conversely, for theology—in its perennial
and ever re-beginning attempts to understand
and to declare for successive cultures
and experience the one eternal revelation
which is the mystery of Christ
—why should theology not ponder, for example,
the *contemporary* passion and darkness of Christ
as found throughout the faithful,
but especially in the 'dark nights'
of the great saints
(whose experiences are *ecclesial*
and for the sake of the whole people of God)
in its effort to understand and declare,
for our time,

the one continuing paschal enterprise
which is human history
as revealed and hoped for in Christian faith?

And this approach could be broadened to a wide range of the *social* and *political,* as well as the more hidden and personal, experience of God's people.[24]

Our final consideration on the contemplation of Christ concerns that third implication of our title, where the contemplative prayer of the Christian receives its structure and impulse,

not so much from Christ himself as object of prayer,
as from Christ's own contemplation of God.

Some modern theology is not without a certain careless christocentrism—almost a christism— which risks subsuming all transcendence either in humanity as such, or at least in the humanity of Christ. This, of course, is death to the specifically religious impulse (though not necessarily the ethical impulse—a related but very different thing).[25] Indeed,

the humanity of Christ is relevant as religious,
and is therefore the permanently proper concern
of contemplative prayer,

precisely because it is revelatory
of the *Godhead,*
which *alone* is proportioned
to the graced desires of man's heart.

The contemplation of Christ
—therefore our contemplation of him
as well as his own contemplation—
is not fully itself as a religious and human act
until, in and through Christ,
it opens out on God
(as an always incarnational preoccupation,
therefore, with precisely *dis*carnate transcendence).[26]

And it is just here
that the apparent similarity and even identity
of all religious contemplation—Christian
and non-Christian—appears initially suasive,[27]
as if Christ were a symbol or story one outgrows
or a grossness which mature contemplation outstrips.

And yet it is also at just this point
that the radical and permanent difference
of Christian contemplation from all other kinds
remains an altogether demonstrable fact
—though a fact of faith alone, to be sure.[28]

And the difference is Christ,
and in his full density as history.

For the God *beyond* Christ
of Christian contemplative prayer
is the precise God *of* Christ.
And we would not know his name—it is Father—
except it were revealed to us in Christ.
And we only know what he has to say
and what, as a matter of fact, he has cared to do,
because this word to us and this deed for us

is Christ
—and nothing else.

Father Rahner has seen this clearly in the distinctions he draws between nature mysticism, metaphysical or philosophical mysticism, and Christian mysticism.[29] In nature mysticism the contemplative existentializes—experiences—the truth of his acknowledgment of God 'as ground of the world' and as 'the ultimate background of everything we meet as man and world in its own reality'. Here it may even seem as though man and the world are the *raison d'etre* of God, at least of the God who shows himself and insofar as he can show himself in the world'. However, where metaphysics is not only theoretically allowed but also existentializes itself as religious experience, 'at the same time' as the fact that God

> appears to us as the ground of the world and the world as the meaning of God, we come to know him as the free, personal, in himself eternal being and thereby as the God beyond the world and all finitude, so that the world does not properly express what he is and may be as the personal and free and eternal being. The world does not reveal to us the *raison d'etre* of God.

And then Rahner moves on to our point:

> But with that, the human . . . question of God has already terminated in an essential failure: it is faced with a free Person closed in on himself, the God who covers himself in silence . . . And what this infinite God is in himself, and how this free personal God wants perhaps, as is possible, to deal with us, this question which for all its obscurity is decisive for our existence cannot be illuminated by the natural light of reason (or by nature mysticism or metaphysical mysticism either). Whether he wants to meet us immediately and personally, whether he wants to remain silent, what he will say to us if he does want to speak—all this is an essential mystery . . . for every impetus of man's passionate desire to know, which originates in the world. So in itself . . . (the human) would have to conclude in an eternally watchful readiness of man to keep his ear cocked in case this distant, silent He should will to speak, in a readiness for the perhaps possible possibility of a revelation.[30]

Revelation: 'the living personal God has spoken to man in Christianity, that is, in Jesus Christ'.[31]

The silent God has spoken,
radically distinguishing Christian mysticism
from every other kind.
The contemplative prayer of a Christian
indeed moves beyond—in and through,
to beyond—the humanity of Christ.
But always to *Christ's* God
—always to the God of Jesus Christ.

Christian contemplation is adoration and obedience
only as a reply to revelation:
a reply to an eternal Word
who is Son, now spoken, for our time, as history
—and to the written, scriptural words
that emerge as integrally one with the event
of his flesh.
And the word is Christ: this is my Son.
And if it is God who gives us Christ
in the shattering terror and hope
of the paschal drama,

it is Christ who gives us God.
We shall never know what God is.
But however dark and deserted,
or however blazing with light and consolation
the crucifying splendors
of contemplative prayer may be,
we do know very well *who* he is:

the Father of our Lord Jesus Christ.

'So when you pray, say Our Father . . .'

Christ is the Word of God. And scripture, in a different but equally serious sense, is also the word of God.[32] Scripture

is the Father,
telling us the story of his Son
—the story of his sons!
It is his own story too,
and neither the gardens of contemplative prayer
nor the deserts of its naked faith
have either need or possibility

of anything or anyone less or other
than the God and Father whom Christ reveals.
It is in Christ alone and 'in the sacred books
(that) the Father who is in heaven
meets his children with great love
and speaks with them'.[33]
And it is in Christ alone,

through the gospel and eucharist
of his continuing ecclesial flesh,

that the Christian contemplative replies.

We conclude these few thoughts with the
remembrance of what we said at the beginning:

that in treating of the contemplation of Christ,
we are dealing with the prayer of a *Christian*.
And a Christian, Paul has superbly told us,
is a life lived in the Spirit
of Father and of Son
—the Spirit whom the johannine Christ
was glorified in death to give.[34]
All is this gift who is Spirit.
It is the Spirit in us who prays:
for it is by the Spirit of God alone
that a man says Jesus is Lord
—and it is by the Spirit of Christ alone
that a man cries 'Abba, Father!'[35]

Contemplation actualizes this trinitarian love life,
which God is,
and for which man is made,
gives it a contemporary history and flesh,

and a world to love.

That world and its mankind
are loved by *man* with *God's* urgency
through the conscious and free appropriation
of the Spirit
which is man's contemplation of the Father
in Christ.

5. Wonder and Contemplation

Wonder and Contemplation: our subject, as we intend to take it, verges on tautology. And this is just as well, for we deal here with a subject deep and huge beyond telling. We meet man in his primal moment as project, process and achievement,

where he greets the real

—God, self, the world and other men—greets it as mystery, and not as information, and long before and forever after ideas, or things, or God, or self, or others, are problematic, analyzed, or used. The latin *mirabilia, mirabilia Dei*—wonders, wonders of God—suggests the english mirror, where the element of objectivity involved, of distance and detachment, is exact.

This argues peremptorily for humility, austerity,
for John the Baptist;
that is, quite literally, for selflessness,
if the real is to have an epiphany consonant
with *its* truth, that is, achieve a new existence
in our consciousness

according to its own otherness and identity
precisely as an unmanipulated self.
Only the imperfections of a mirror announce
its existence when the drama is in play.
And they do so, always, by working darkness
or distortion upon what is contemplated, mirrored,
wondered at.

We are at the roots here of reverence and respect:
action centered in the Other and the others,
according to *their* existence, their goodness,
truth and beauty—and their promise.

Especially promise.
The promise of another
in this weak and splendid unconcluded world
of ours—those signals of a destiny
that just could be triumphant—well, they seed
our growth and ground our hope. But they are spied
at *cost,* since we are prone to sinfulness,
which never takes flesh except as selfishness:
that lapse of contemplation, however momentary,
which is the death of wonder.
We are called to that *attention!*
which lies at the heart of both the gospel [1]
and the monastic 'watch', to that virginal
expectation and alertness for the bridegroom.

Contemplation, then, is vigorous *action,*
which ponders the other—God, man and world—
turning them over in the heart (Mary),
and is the condition of science as well as of art,
of secularity as well as of religion.
It is action centered in the Other and the others,
as we said, according to *their* reality and promise,
their terror and their truth.
And if it is expensive—the market price
of wonder and joy (as opposed to pleasure)
being always a death to selfishness—
it may well be thought worth the price and risk.
For if reality—God, man and world—is a gift,
if it is simply *there* to be met with in its quality
as unmanipulated, objective and other
—as the example of the mirror suggests—
if we are such a gift *to* each other,
yet nevertheless, and as equally so, we ourselves
are at stake as well. For we are *received*
from another. We are a gift that is given.
We are grace.

Every man is told this profoundly just as soon
as his story begins: we do not name ourselves.
Our name (who shall we be?) is a gift from another.
The recent *Man of La Mancha* is vivid here.
It seizes upon the Christian romance
of contemplation as the totally *unsentimental*
grappling with the real, as it is: not avoiding,
but grasping and keeping company with its weakness
and horror and disappointment;
yet keeping faith too with its wonder
as spied only in *contemplative* gaze.
It is a look that needs to be long and hardy
and faithful, a love-look
that penetrates my promise and creates me,
making my dream come true.

La Mancha dramatizes the mystery
of the biblical theme of the name
and of the changing of the name
as no mere sign or pointer, but as laden with
and creative of the *ding an sich,*
the thing itself.
Quixote calls the prostitute
his lady Dulcinea and, transcending all rejection
with fidelity, invites her, indeed compels her,
by his faithfulness to the beauty that he sees,
to choose in freedom the beauty that she is,
and so become—herself.

The conditions of Don Quixote's creative
contemplation, of his capacity for wonder
—for making dreams just be (that's first),
in order to come true—
are simple and severe: formalized
not especially as introspecting self-perfection,
but rather as ecstasy and extroversion:
action centered in the Other and the others,
that God and world and other men may happen
in their unique and glorious otherness—may happen
for him, Don Quixote—just happen, and be so.

The theme is emphatically marian,
where the project and adventure, fully done,
of contemplation as attentive humility
before reality as grace

explodes on God himself: 'let it happen to me'.

And that was Christ,

who would in turn be wonder-full for history
only to contemplative, unself-regarding faith
(with the romance of the ethics of the Sermon
on the Mount proving steadily, mercifully absurd
and useless, sentimental and unrealistic,
where appropriated in precision from mystery,
sin and grace).

And John the Baptist appears here too,
as forerunner surely, but also as that perennial
companion and ingredient of the real
that must also sponsor, if it is to be well met by,
the contemplative heart.
For granted that we do love,
that we do take a very good look (contemplate),
and that we do serve,
yet we are always just about to, too.
The situation of contemplation endures
only in continuing obedience to John's rude
and accurate advice: before you do anything else,
just get yourself out of the way.
That kind of poverty, emptiness of self,
which the child is and which Job finally learned,
is the preface and the permanent comrade
of wonder.

In leaving Quixote, Mary and the Baptist,

we ought to consider how far their reality—even as scarcely touched on here—has nevertheless blatantly outstripped our thought of them. For we looked at their truth to see how wonder is and arises (in its own aftermath as awe) out of that reverent, respectful occupation with the real, in *its* otherness, interiority and promise. And we gathered from both Mary and Quixote how this contemplation, where well done, is not only carefully, literally reflective, but is also essentially creative and actualizing of the other's reality and promise (Christ and Dulcinea).[2] Finally, in the Baptist we are met with the constant, negative condition of all human personality as contemplative surrender:

that death
of the petty scattered, having self

which manipulates and squanders the real,
dominating rather than adoring
that which is,[3]
corrupting rather than serving
that which ought to be.[4]

Yet at least two further, polar truths stand patent already from our examples, and they are equally interior and fundamental to the being of contemplation and wonder as those truths we have remarked. The first is clear in its simple, splendid statement. If it is the case that a young girl, precisely as contemplative,

is so creative of the God she ponders
that he becomes history as Christ,
yet equally and even more entirely
does this woman come to be as Mary
through this adventure and event.

And if the errant knight's reverent,
intransigently loving contemplation
of the prostitute is evocation and even *deed*
of her as Dulcinea,
yet we are also witness here, in that victorious
dialectic of all successful contemplation,
to a giant stride and penetration
into that noble dream and promise
that shall come true as Don Quixote.

The objects of contemplation, then,
are also creative of their lover.

And wonder, as man's loss of self in the other,
as his ardent *moving out* into the others and Other,
is also man's arrival upon himself as man.
Precisely as contemplative servant
of the real—God, fellow men and the world—

man happens, he occurs, he is man.

Where this is done at all, there is personality.
Where it is well done and with fidelity,
there is sanctity.

A second truth, and also fully explicit from the beginning of our reflection on contemplation and wonder, causes our example of the mirror to founder on a beauty to which it cannot respond. Wonder as mirror, we saw, answers forcefully to the objective character, the otherness and 'thereness'—to the gift-and-grace quality, of reality. The example leads, therefore,

to reverence and respect.
It asks for careful humility in judgment
and invites us to be surprised.
This is indispensable to awe and amazement,
those precious attributes of wonder
which a man may feel before the simplest flower,
the hands of a friend,
or almighty God

—if he will *really* look
(it is not easy),
with a passion for the evidence,
for the *facts* of the real, and with a disposition
to respond according to what is *given* him to see.
It ought not be assumed that such honesty is easy,
and that all difficulty focuses on responding
to what we see.
The 'doors of perception' [5] are cleansed
with labor and humility,
as Darwin learned in searching for the data
in order that reality might be for man

—simply be itself.

Initially and finally, the doors are cleansed
by grace. We ask,
and we are given—we are even given to ask—
not to be deaf and blind.

Yet having stressed that objective element of contemplation which gives to it its first dignity —especially in the case of friendship and of God— and where the example of the mirror may survive, it yet remains paramount, radically intrinsic to the enterprise of wonder, and constitutive of the final excitement of contemplative knowledge as love, that the registration of the object in question

is on *human freedom*
and not on glass—on human freedom,
whose active, contributing, creative character

is properly at the very forefront
of every discussion of the human.
Contemplation and wonder

are *action* centered in the other.

That is, contemplative knowledge
is born of, as well as fruitful of, love.
It is in my freedom's *appropriation*
of what yet remains sheer gift
that there occurs on the frontiers of contemplative
encounter that *inter*-action with the other
which, whether abruptly, or slowly
and after the grain dies,
fissions to the paradox of wonder: *both*
intimacy and distance, *both* tenderness
and reverence,

both fascination and holy fear.

We catch the full tension of this action and passion,
this intimacy and mystery—and we recall the theme
of the name—in the book of Genesis where Jacob
encounters God; wrestles him to earth; prevails;
is named anew as Israel; concludes: 'Tell me *your*
name', and has his reply: 'Why do you ask my
name?' [6]

In the knowledge: mystery.
In the intimacy: awe.

Children instruct us fundamentally and movingly,
if initially and somewhat superficially,
in the matter of contemplation;
and they warn us against the death of wonder.
The inaugural simplicity of the human heart
is celebrated in the child's wide-eyed rush
to the light, to the flower, to whatever is new,
revealed and there

—especially to the thunder heard
in the quiet of a smile.

The eyes grow big, the hands reach out
—and stop, reverently. And the touch is chaste.
There is delight, total involvement, not a shred
of self—and silence,

until the cry of wonder.
The eyes turn to the adult. And the questions
are: what, and why.

The beautiful and the holy are very near.

Yet the capacity dims most often, and the question
turns into: what for, and, does it work.
This is not defeat,

but the larger task lies ahead now: not in the
refusal of these last concerns (they are the basis
of much good science, secularity and incarnationalism),
but in the *penetration* of the pragmatic, the handled,
and the familiar

on down deep to the *roots* of particularity
where everything is new and wonderful,
and strange as God.[7]
Here lies the ambitious, Christian childhood
of the gospel
that only the adult can manage.

The task is beset with problems which, like most
others, admit of false solutions—untruths difficult
to work with often, because partially, even largely,
true. In the first line of vision, though, lies a
stunning truth, and it is evil:

all our historical and contemporary brothers
and sisters who have never been allowed to wonder.
It is the primal theft:

the theft of childhood
—at any age.

And its means are both gross and subtle.
For we bludgeon one another, individually
and as societies and cultures—we bludgeon
one another's capacity to dream and will
the beautiful,
whether with a violence as sophisticated
as advertising, or with the cruder forms
of violence such as poverty, regimentation,
racism and war.
So that many of our brothers have no time
—no real, psychological, spiritual, *human* time
and space and peace—for wonder and contemplation.

We do it to our children, our parents,
our friends.
And as this or that man or community crosses
the physical or cultural or spiritual poverty-line,
we 'raise the ante' constantly.

We enslave one another with the need to *have*
as a condition of becoming,
while always postponing the moment of *being,*
self-surrender, wonder and praise.
Yet 'how much leisure and pay is the miner to have,
till he is to be taught to love prayer
and the thought of God?'
And there is a similar question for those
rightly busy in seeking the miner's justice.[8]

A second problem is suggested here by 'those rightly busy in seeking the miner's justice'. And the issue often gets canonized in a famous phrase that is sometimes (and pretty fairly) proposed as a summary of the spirituality of Ignatius of Loyola:

finding God in all things.

The presupposition here, of course,
is biblically and dogmatically immaculate:
God *is* in all things (though not equally so,
unless pantheistic humanism is the point).
But *finding* God in all things,

meeting and greeting *him* there

—and the conditions of that—
is another, surely deeply related,
but perhaps slightly more complex affair.
And wonder, wonder at God just here,
is what is at stake, together with what
is organically and not peripherally involved
in such wonder:

man's coming to be as man
through conscious, immediate encounter with God.

The conditions of the numinous, of wonder,
are severe,
as we already know from John the Baptist:

awe and amazement, reverence and respect,
humility and gratitude, service and self-effacement,
will test the presence of the Holy One.
The case is especially pressing
in the matter of reform.
Only contemplative love shall act re-creatively,
rather than routinely, cleverly,
and on the surface. For only love gives life.
The implications are ominous in reformers
who do not contemplate—and superb in those who do—
contemplate the *mystery* of the papacy, of celibacy,
America, or of anything or anyone at all.

Reform, at its own peril,
must pause for celebration,
and for the giving of great thanks.

To tackle mystery in the first place as a problem
is a sin.[9]

There is a temptation, further, in the adage, finding God in all things, which has a large and contemporary history. And it is twofold. The temptation suggests, first of all,

that we identify contemplation and action,
neatly and without remainder.
That identity, to be sure, is God's situation,
and it is strongly characteristic,
not of the contemplation (which always seems
to survive as itself), but of the action
of the saints in their maturity.
Yet it speaks to a harmony that we,
poor sinful men and as spirit-in a-body-in-the-world,
are largely always on the way to,
both in our love for God and one another,
and in our encounter with the ideas and things
of our historical existence.

Idolatry—which is to have and use
instead of serve each other and our world—
is the death of wonder and threatens all involvement
that is not *reverent* intimacy.
We must really look—take a very good look—
at the sheer otherness before us:
whether a flower, an idea, or a friend

and see what is there,
and how we are to serve its promise.

This is to love what *God* sees and has in mind
for our brothers and our world.
And that takes time, habits of fresh perception,
detachment, freedom from the other *for* the other;
that poverty of self that allows us, frees us
to notice—especially in the case of the familiar—
one another's beauty and hope,

and to be surprised.

The temptation of the adage, finding God in all things, secondly concerns the *structure* of our contemplation of God, each other and our world. This touches on the sources of wonder, for the temptation suggests that we come to God *only* in and through creatures, that is, by ardent, dedicated involvement with our fellow men and the material world alone. 'Christ is other people'—taken absolutely—is another, even more limiting expression (since it does not even hope to move on to Christ himself) of the same stance.

The first thing to notice about this position is the difficulty of finding any saint who espouses it. That Jesus did not do so is usually granted without much question, though the anthropological framework within which he had to live and work may get cited as excusing cause for his direct preoccupation with the Father.[10] That Ignatius of Loyola did not do so either may be gathered *inter alia* just from that consideration—easily considered pedestrian—in the *Spiritual Exercises,* where he discusses that common phenomenon of his own day: oath-taking. The *less* perfect man ought to swear, if swear he must, by God alone, since the respect due to God will be immediately obvious. Only the *more* perfect should swear by creatures, and for the splendid reason that they are more likely to have that *reverence* and care —that attitude of wonder—toward creatures that will discern how they have come from God, are coming from his hand at just this moment, and are destined for him alone.[11] The descending movement of all Ignatian theology and contemplation is clear and well documented. Ignatius moves from God to the world, and never the other way about.[12] The *Spiritual*

Exercises are rooted in the divine as initiative, and not as term only. Indeed they have their beginning, middle and end in a Father who wishes to deal *directly* with the one who makes the exercises.[13]

The incarnation of God in Jesus Christ,
of course, radically reinterprets and creates anew
the meaning of the world
and of all social, cultural, material existence.
The incarnation is a permanent announcement
that God not only may, but as a matter of fact,
does, choose our fellow men and our world
as the place and time
in which he wishes to greet us and be served.
But the structure of this incarnationalism
is exposed: it is in the contemplation of *God*
that the world is discovered as given by God,
as coming from God,
and as going to God;
and *then* arises the cry of wonder:

God, found in all things!

And the anti-humanist charge falls well short here.
For there is no question in incarnationalism
of loving God alone,
or even of also loving others quite directly
but only for God's sake.
Rather, the adventure

is to love *all* God loves (a world and a world of men),
as God loves it (directly and in detail:
the hairs on our heads and the sparrows), and
with his love (that is, in his world-affirming Spirit).

This last establishes the place of contemplation
as intrinsic to Christian humanism
as action in the world.
And to love the world with God's love
is never to fail in reverence and wonder.

But it takes a man alive
with *God's* fidelity to do this:

to love our fellow men, in all their need
—espying the beauty of their promise
and persisting—through to the end.

The source of friendship as wonder,
and of secularity too,
is the contemplation of God.

It is important too to see here, in connection with incarnationalism, that revelation, especially in its fullness as the trinitarian epiphany of God in Christ, further declares, spells out and gives flesh to—and that it never, in any way, attenuates—God's mystery. And fidelity to contemplation of the gospels, to frequentation of the sacraments and to other religious practices—while running the risk (as everything human, including friendship, does) of a familiarity which breeds boredom, routine and the search for that novelty which marks the death of wonder: nevertheless such fidelity has very much the opposite intention as its graced dynamism, wherever *contemplation,* and not its counterfeits (mere dreaming, or the cult of experience), survives and intensifies.

For contemplation, wonder, are love.
And love is work—a grace and a gift
to be fought for, through effort and training
and habits and tears,
with fidelity, through to the end.

For if the eye stays clear (John the Baptist),
then the ceaselessly new disclosure (grace)
and discovery (freedom)
both of *what* the mystery is
and of how *mysterious* it is,
is as inevitable as the beloved's
own inexhaustibility,
and will therefore be productive
of ever greater amazement and awe.

All theology, and scientific scripture studies too, have their final purpose identified and tested here.

Do they *serve* the real, laying bare the integral,
always unfashionable mystery (ever old and new)
and rendering it ever more available
for that wonder which issues in the action
that is adoration and obedience?

Further, it may be noticed that *all* science, where formally engaged in as human, precisely in its pragmatism has contemplation and wonder, and not pragmatism, as its final intention and criterion.

For man is made for joy and self-surrender,
for poverty and being,
and not for pleasure, or for having,
or for self-fulfilment either
—these latter being by-products,
if the former are well done.

The Trinity instructs us here.
For it is the Father's total poverty
and contemplation, it is his moving *out*
into the Son, which gives the Son
his entire existence and his name.
Yet it is exactly the existence of the Son,
as Son, and nothing else, which constitutes
the Father in his reality as Father.
The reality of God, then, its explanation
and its judgment on itself, are one:
faithful love.
And the unity of the Godhead, as *one*
precisely in the real *distinction* of its Persons,
captures

the *reverent intimacy*

which is contemplation
and which signals the presence of wonder.

Perhaps man knows this best, if largely wordlessly, in the mystery that is friendship. We shall bring these unsystematic reflections to a close, then, by considering the role of contemplation and wonder in the rigorous joy of friends.[14] The case is impressive, as we said, beyond the resources of language, or thought either, to deliver.

We take to the road in acquaintanceship,[15]
where the element of choice seems large:
I may choose my friends.
Later, when the relationship emerges
as more fully itself—or fails to—the naiveté
of this will be clear. For love is a gift.
And while I may reject it, I may not compel it.

This is fairly easy to see, when it happens,
in the element of *being* loved.
Yet grace is equally true of the love I give.
That must be given me too. I am *given* to love
by the beauty I perceive. For the beauty of another
actuates my promise as a lover, even as my love
calls forth the beautiful to being.
Herein we have the basic dialectic of contemplation
as both action and passion,
as totally grace, and utterly free.
Infatuation, compulsion, therefore, are ruled out:
they are something else,
and diriment impediments to friendship.

Wonder attends the story's start,
and constant, easy surprise.
Contemplation (which really need only be glancing
to succeed at this point) is smooth,
undistracted and winning,
where the going is good and mutual.
Novelty fuels each encounter, freshness
is everywhere, and ardent ease.
The illusion of forever is palpable.
It is acquaintanceship still, and resembles
the child's wonder: often brilliant,
yet as often phosphorescent
—with the resources of fidelity untested.

Then surface novelty ends.
Minds have been explored, histories shared,
and personalities indulged. At that level
where men live who do not contemplate,
now there is nothing 'new'.
Boredom, however cordial, is in sight.
And death—whatever the social rubrics
of 'keeping in touch'—may ensue.
It may well go unmourned, where nothing
quite final and joyful, but only entertainment,
'relevance' and 'interest' were ever alive.

We rarely weep
except where we have really wondered.

Circumstances can mask all this. For at this point,
factors such as work, or living-situation, or children,
financial security, or just sheer habit, may suggest
or even require that the companionship survive the

juncture we are at. For a summer, for years, or even for a lifetime.

The relationship gets announced for what it is more clearly where there are no such circumstances which, on their own account, foster or even demand the companionship.

The relationship of love must *choose* itself now,
and *decide* upon fidelity.
Usually we do not do so, whether out of fear
of the desert and the darkness
that all love involves,
or because we simply have no idea
—because no experience to go by—that we are,
as a matter of fact, just on the threshold
of our own and another's mystery.
Israel was appalled to discover
that the journey out of Egypt—initiated,
we remember, with all wonder and delight—
could possibly involve the drabness of the desert
and that literally awful encounter
with her *own* truth and with the other's truth
which loving with fidelity always exacts.
We forfeit joy, of course, when we refuse
this march into another, this invasion by another
—joy:

> that privileged heart of wonder
> reserved to mystery *engaged* in.

But we also spare ourselves the agony
of the journey, and the boredom of loitering,
indefinitely and almost as a way of life,
at the threshold of surprise.
Rather we elect that spiritual promiscuity,
so often praised as openness to experience
and to growth, which draws lines,
which settles for brief excursions,
and so moves from one 'friendship' to another,
and another—and once more.
Wonder here has settled for excitement
and will never know

> the awe of single-eyed fidelity,
> at any cost.

One may well ask why one should cross

such deserts and such mountains,
and whether permanent commitment of this kind
is real at all (the charge of narrowness
is famous) and, if so, worth the price.
But just to place this question
is already to stand outside the context
of its answer.

For love can appeal to nothing beyond itself.

As one stands at this juncture
where novelty declines and where love
fully enters into itself as formal choice
and decision and *will,*
one either dreams, or one does not.
Dreams are not always idle.
They are also a creative judgment about the real.
Concerning both man's adventure into God
and man's adventure into man:
how much is there to know, what is there to love?

Man as *contemplative*
rather than as discursive freedom
is the lapidary issue here.

The decision to press the evidence (yet always
in terms of it) and to contemplate the loved one
without presupposition or condition,
simply forces the matter of fidelity.
It is a time for heart.
But neither the question nor the reality
of fidelity may ever be separated
from contemplation and wonder,
as if asceticism were a task for itself.
For the fidelity of friendship
is dialectically born out of that wonder
which contemplation of the loved one is.
And the converse is equally so:
out of the beauty seen and loved
arises the élan for faithful service
to the future pursuit of beauty's promise.

Perhaps the path could,
but it need not here, be further mapped.
Rocky hope. Rugged peace. Laughter.
And silence.

Any decent manual of prayer—not to mention the

memoirs of the great mystical lovers of God in Christ
—details a similar story:

the birth of love in wonder and delight,
together with the grief
that one has come so sinful, scattered
and so unprepared
to this moment one had waited all one's life for;
then the journey into the desert,
largely undramatic (this is important)—perhaps
even unnoticed where the friend,
and not the filing away of self, is concentrated on;
and finally,

on to the adventurous peace of daily-ness
where everything is new,
quietly superb, thoroughly unnaive,
yet simple and strong as a child
whose innocence is undefeated.
It is the gospel childhood of the adult.
A preview and inauguration of the Kingdom
which makes all things new.
Arrived at not without scars

—but they are beautiful now.

By definition, friendship as *contemplative* love
is not blind, but wholly intent on the truth
that is there and that ought to be
—alert to the detail of the other.
And while such love is never critical
or unaccepting,
yet it is, silently, productive of noble shame
and peremptorily imperative of the other's
best self in freedom.
The joke that love is blind
in finding the beloved beautiful is faulted here.

For contemplation is the art of the real.
And the real *is* beautiful:
it is what God has in mind,
and that is always lovely.

A friend is the one—perhaps the only one—
who really begins to see what God sees.
The *contemplative* judgment of a friend
may stand with confidence against the world.

The language of this love and wonder is restrained,
as are its gestures.
Words may say all, or nearly so, of an acquaintance,
but they point, and grope, then shatter
in the presence of mystery.
Awe grows large here, as doubt vanishes.
Awe and skepticism are intrinsically opposites,
and wordless amazement
is the deep contrary of uncertainty (a truth
theology always needs to ponder).

Take the man who replies about his friend
to a mutual acquaintance: 'Yes, that's true.
And that, yes, that's accurate enough too.
But it's not really it. No, that's not it. Well,
I don't know. I really don't know *what* to say.'
It is the learned ignorance of love
we overhear in this.
It is wonder: that contemplative wisdom
that is not thought and cannot speak,
the *docta ignorantia* of the Fathers of the Church
and of the mystics. John of the Cross
records it of his love affair with God:
that greatest gift of loving God so much
that we know we do not know him at all.

Yet also and conversely,
the experience of friendship, of contemplative love,
is *merciful* to language, and to gesture too:
it renews, gives new mint to,
the familiar and the misused,
the carelessly given word and embrace.
For it scours the lover, re-creates him.
Its forgiveness gives innocence
and a new beginning
to words that were spoken without contemplation
and to hands that touched without love.

This love of friendship, where authentically itself,
is never introvert—an *égoisme à deux*—
but is always inclusive of the third.
And this openness to others
tests every friendship as certainly and absolutely
as the ethics of the Sermon on the Mount
judge the contemplative love
of every Christian mystic.

For the more deeply both these loves
seek their own undissipated being,
the more fully will community occur.

Again, the Trinity instructs us:
it is the *totality* of the mutual self-surrender
in love of Father and of Son
which *is* the Person of the Holy Spirit.
And this is a truth that short-circuits any notion
of friendship as a luxury.
Its products are *love* and so must appear primary
on any list of the necessities of a life
that is human and Christian.

Contemplation, to conclude,
is chaste and reverent passion for the real
—whether God, our fellow men, or the world.
It is a deed that takes a lifetime,
and is not easily done.
Where done well and with fidelity,
across deserts and maybe some sandstorms,
through to the end,
it is productive of the literally wonderful:

> that love and joy which God is
> and for which man is made.

The lesson is clear,
if this is the case: friendship is grace.
For—to repeat ourselves—

> it takes a man alive with *God's* fidelity

to see really and to love wholly
his fellow man in all his need,
through to the end where beauty bides as wonder,
asking to be born.

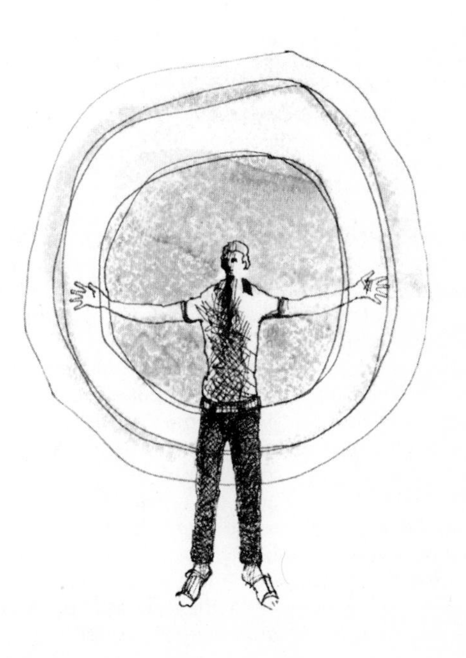

NOTES

Preface

1. The story of Benjamin is told in Gen 28—45.

2. '. . . Unless the grain falls into the ground and dies . . .' See Jn 12.24.

3. See *Contra Faustum*, xxii, 52, 58. The relevant passages may be found in Butler, Cuthbert, *Western Mysticism*, London, 1922; 3rd edition, 1967, pp. 159–60.

4. Both works are dated somewhere between 1153 and 1162, the *Benjamin Minor* being the earlier of the two. For the salient passages in this treatise, see pp. 77ff. in *Richard of Saint-Victor, Selected Writings on Contemplation*, translated with introduction by Clare Kirchberger, New York, 1957.

5. *A Treatise of the Study of Wisdom that Men Call Benjamin.* The treatise is cited and described in Johnston, William, *The Mysticism of the Cloud of Unknowing*, New York, 1967, esp. pp. 127–31.

6. The theme of Benjamin as contemplation also gets developed through the medieval mis-reading of the text of Psalm 67.27 (or 68.28) where 'Benjamin, the least of them (the tribes), in the lead', was mistakenly read as 'Benjamin, a youth, in ecstasy of mind'.

7. Even given their insufficient perspective on the human as historical, the scholastics were very good on this relation of rational, conceptual knowledge (Rachel), intuitive knowledge (Joseph, roughly speaking), and wisdom, taken as that knowledge which is born of as well fruitful of *love* (Benjamin). Within not a few of the chiselled scholastic formulae there lurks a rich experience that is far more Christian than Greek. For the experience finally remains true to that fundamental gospel criticism of the view that the will necessarily follows the intellect. That criticism may be expressed in the words of Jesus: 'Blessed are the pure of heart, they shall see God.' This essentially extrovert, contemplative insight gets classic, if paradoxical, statement in the aphorism of William of Saint-Thierry: 'Amor ipse intellectus est'.

Chapter I Faith and Hope and Love

1. 1 Cor 12-13.

2. 1 Thess 5.8, 1.3, and see Rom 5.1-5, 1 Cor 13.13, Col 1.4-5, and compare Heb 10.21-25.

3. Rom 8.9-17, 1 Cor. 2.10-13.

4. Rom 8.18-26.

5. Gal 2.20, Acts 17.28, 2 Cor 1.20.

6. Lk 2.

7. 1 Cor 15.24-28.

8. See 1 Cor 15.19.

9. 1 Cor 16.21, Apoc 22.20.

10. 1 Pet 3.15.

11. Heb 6.18-19.

12. Col 3.1-4.

13. Lk 24.21.

14. Heb 13.8, 1 Cor 15.17.

15. Eph 2.12.

Chapter II Salvation through Suffering

1. Suffering: that is, an *allowing*, which can be a very active affair that seminally marshals freedom—as the successful experience of *being* loved attests.

Chapter III Prayer and Religion

1. Von Hügel (1825-1925) was a married lay theologian who figured prominently in the 'modernist' movement and crisis. He enjoyed an international reputation in philosophy, biblical studies, ecumenism and mystical theology. All our unacknowledged citations are from him. His major works include: *The Mystical Element of Religion, Eternal Life, Essays and Addresses on the*

Philosophy of Religion (2 series). For a fuller study of prayer and religion in von Hügel, see Whelan, Joseph P., *The Spirituality of Friedrich von Hügel*, London, 1971.

2. Guardini, Romano, *Prayer in Practice*, New York, 1963, p. 153. My italics.

3. See below, Chapter 4, note 3.

4. Clearly, the term 'religion' here does not answer to the usage of some modern German theologians, e.g. Barth and Bonhoeffer. The term here speaks also and indeed primarily of man's relationship with God and of God's relationship with man, and not merely of man's possible ways (whether legitimate or idolatrous) of acting out, or dramatizing, or even of controlling or domesticating, that relationship.

5. 'Normal' here distinctly does not say 'frequent', or 'widespread'. And herein, I would think, lies one of the major issues for modern man to discern about himself and his culture.

6. Jn 14.23, Apoc 22.17, 20.

Chapter IV Contemplating Christ

1. See Heiler, Friedrich, *Prayer*, Oxford, 1932, and Bernard, Charles, *La Prière Chrétienne*, Bruges, 1967. And see above, Chapter 3, note 4.

2. See Chapter 3.

3. Bernard, *op. cit.*, and Nédoncelle, Maurice, *God's Encounter with Man*, New York, 1964. For Bernard, pp. 33-35 and *passim*, all prayer is 'une mise en presence', and 'relations inter-personnelles' are the 'elément décisif'—the one common denominator of *all* forms of prayer, which underlies and outstrips all language and every concept.

4. This character of prayer as inter-personal relationship is, of course, much discussed and questioned today. Its importance for the very existence of *prayer* (as differentiated from meditation or reflection) is not easily overstressed (see references in notes 1 and 3 above).

5. Guardini, *op. cit.*, is excellent on this question of recollection, of 'collectedness'.

6. See Chapter 3.

7. See von Balthasar, Hans Urs, 'Theology and Sanctity', in *Word and Redemption*, New York, 1965.

8. Ruysbroeck, *The Adornment of Spiritual Marriage, II*, cited in Merton, Thomas, *Contemplative Prayer*, New York, 1969, p. 102.

9. See Merton, *ibid.*

10. See especially Hosea, and Ezekiel 16.

11. Yet this eternal structure (which is the one revelation), in gaining a new historical existence, also achieves a quite novel conformation each time this sacred history encounters, shapes, and gets shaped by, the individual and communal psychology, culture, body, etc. of the contemplative himself and of the larger community with whom he interacts. It acquires, of course, its most significant continuing incarnation, not in the determinisms of psychology, environment, etc., but in the *freedom* and *love* with which the contemplative utilizes these materials in entering the paschal darkness and light of his own faith experience and that of his fellow men.

12. Apoc 5.6.

13. I have been helped in this point by Stanley, David, 'Contemplation of the Gospels and the Contemporary Christian', in *Prayer: The Problem of Dialogue with God*, edited by Christopher Mooney, New Jersey, 1969 and also printed in *Theological Studies*, September, 1968.

14. Bernard, *op. cit., passim.*

15. See, e.g. Eph 1.

16 A point vigorously made by Teresa of Avila.

17. Fitzmyer, Joseph, handles this whole question masterfully and economically in 'The Spiritual Exercises of Saint Ignatius and Recent Gospel Study', in *Woodstock Letters*, vol. 91, no 3.

18. See von Balthasar, 'The Place of Theology', *op. cit.*

19. Once again, on this whole point, I am immensely indebted to David Stanley, *art. cit.*

20. See Rom 1.4 and Acts 2.36.

21. Heb 13.8.

22. This is a staple of pauline contemplative prayer. See e.g. 2 Cor 5.17, Phil 3.7-9 and Gal 2.19-20. The whole question is well treated in Wikenhauser, Alfred, *Pauline Mysticism*, New York, 1960.

23. In 'Theology and Sanctity', *op. cit.*, p. 80. My italics.

24. *Ibid.* It should be noticed, however, that belief and holiness are presuppositions, *just here*, of such material's being available to theology.

25. See Chapter 3.

26. *Ibid.*

27. This very common position gets well stated in its general form by Huxley, Aldous, *The Doors of Perception*, New York, 1963. Huxley is directly replied to in Zaehner, R. C., *Mysticism Sacred and Profane*, New York, 1967.

28. This statement is intentionally forceful. It does not want to advocate stalemate in inter-denominational or inter-religious dialogue. Rather it wants to keep such dialogue hard-edged, that is, in touch with the specific, concrete *detail* of actual religious experience—detail that pertains to the substance and not just to the mode of such experience.

29. Rahner, Karl, 'The Ignatian Mysticism of Joy in the World', in *Theological Investigations*, Vol. III, Baltimore, 1967.

30. *Ibid.*, p. 284.

31. *Ibid.*, p. 283.

32. There is without question today a problem—which is not this essay's subject—about scripture as the word of God in a serious, unique, quite non-metaphorical sense. Naiveté is never in order. But *simplicity* in the face of one's own present exegetical, form-critical, cultural knowledge, etc. and a *deep faith* in the incarnational possibility and suitability of God the Father's employment of the psychology and pluralist experience of the primitive community and of the several evangelists to declare as *his own* the story of

his Son (just as he made and makes his own the flesh of Jesus of Nazareth and the eucharistic bread) is a *sine qua non* of any success. At any rate, it may be thought that, however different in other ways, the structure and the radical conditions of possibility of scripture as word of God are not different from those which attend the divinity of Jesus or the Real Presence in the Eucharist.

33. *Dei Verbum* ('Constitution on Divine Revelation' of Vatican II), 21.

34. See Jn 14 and 16.

35. See I Cor 12, Gal 4 and Rom 8.

Chapter V Wonder and Contemplation

1. See Gethsemane: 'watch and pray'.

2. Just a glance here suggests that the quality of any society's secular *action* stands in direct, not inverse, proportion to the quality of that society as contemplative. The contemplative point, therefore, is significantly prior to and wider than its fuller and deeper application to inter-personal relationships or to religion as such.

3. Often defended by an appeal to history, or even to all reality, as *simply* process, where nothing *is* except as becoming.

4. Sometimes defended by the view that man creates himself and his world absolutely rather than, as with Jesus, also exercising creative lordship precisely as a servant.

5. Blake, William, *The Marriage of Heaven and Hell.*

6. Gen 33.24-29.

7. See 1 Jn 1.1-4, and so much of Hopkins' poetry. And see Flannery O'Connor, who writes in consistent awe of the deeply familiar as incarnational detail.

8. See Chapter 3.

9. These remarks are based on an article of mine, 'Credibility and Joy', *The Month*, February, 1969.

10. See the splendid, God-centered portrait of Jesus in the

opening pages of Niebuhr, H. Richard, *Christ and Culture*, New York, 1951.

11. See *Spiritual Exercises*, nos. 38-39.

12. See Rahner, Hugo, *Ignatius the Theologian*, London, 1968, Chapter 1; and Rahner, Karl, *op. cit.*, pp. 277-93; also *Spiritual Exercises*, e.g. no. 184.

13. See *Spiritual Exercises*, nos. 5, 15. No. 169 speaks of persons who 'do not go straight to God but want God to come straight to their . . . attachments' (trans. by Joseph Rickaby).

14. I would certainly include, but would in no way limit these remarks to, that friendship which is successful marriage.

15. I am not especially concerned here to criticize acquaintanceship, which may well have its necessary and proper place in human life. I am talking about something else. Indeed, most of us cannot manage many friendships. And while it is indispensable to admire wonder and contemplation—to find them wonderful—it serves no purpose to over-estimate the realistic and graced *range* of our capacity to do it well.